I almost never went to confession at St. Procopius. It was much easier psychologically to go in a different parish, where the priest didn't know you. When you had to tell a priest that you had pressed against Darlene Hollenback's hip for twelve blocks on a crowded bus, you didn't want to have to look him in the eye the next day. Once when I had French-kissed somebody, I bicycled all the way out to St. Boniface's because I was sure nobody there knew me. When I was leaving the confessional, the priest—I still don't know who he was— said, "Say, Tommy, would you open the window before you go?"

Coming soon from Pinnacle Books—
the hilarious sequel to
ONCE A CATHOLIC . . .

ALWAYS A CATHOLIC

Once
A
Catholic

A novel by
Robert
Byrne

PINNACLE BOOKS   NEW YORK

ONCE A CATHOLIC was originally published by that distinguished gentleman and great publisher, Lyle Stuart, under the title *Memories of a Non-Jewish Childhood.*

ONCE A CATHOLIC

A Pinnacle Books edition, published by special arrangement with the author.

First printing, July 1981

ISBN: 0-523-41165-0

Cover illustration by John Solie

Printed in the United States of America

PINNACLE BOOKS, INC.
1430 Broadway
New York, New York 10018

To Pooey, Gooch, Obie, Albo, Juney, Robby, Pete, and Ding, who kept my childhood moving.

Once a Catholic

CHAPTER ONE

1

Normally my mother had to resort to violence to get me out of bed, but one morning I was on my feet dressing with the first rays of the sun. In only forty-five minutes I would make my debut as an altar boy in the big church, having completed the initiation of serving a dozen early Masses in the nuns' chapel. I should have been dreading the mistakes I was bound to make but I was too excited over something else for that. My mind was filled with visions of an event I had been looking forward to for months—this was the day that Porky Schornhorst would light a fart.

Porky Schornhorst lit farts just once a year and only for his closest friends. He was the only person in Dubuque County who could do it or even had the nerve to try. For the first time I was sure that I would be allowed to watch. Not only was I in the eighth grade at St. Procopius and deserving of respect on that account, but Porky lately had been letting me hang around with him and his gang even though most of them were a couple of grades ahead of me.

I suppose there were other kids in the United States who lit farts, but I had no way of knowing about them. To me Porky loomed as one of the two most heroic figures in the world—a world that was more or less bounded on the north by Winona, Minnesota, where my cousin Kathleen was a postulant in the Order of the Blessed Assumption; on the south by Keokuk, Iowa, where my Uncle Vernon had a fine position with the maintenance crew of Lock and Dam Number 38; on the west by Maquoketa, Iowa, where a former neighbor had recently married a non-Catholic; and on the east by Dickeyville, Wisconsin, where a priest had spent a lifetime building an intricate grotto of plaster, colored rocks, pieces of glass, and broken crockery.

The other hero in my life was my brother, Pfc. Paul Shannon, who had swept across North Africa, captured Sicily, and was now occupying Naples with Mark Clark and the rest of the United States Fifth Army. I sometimes caught myself hoping that the Axis could hold on until I was old enough to enlist and fight at his side.

The first noises I heard that morning were heavy grindings and scrapings from the basement, where my mother was fixing the furnace, and the first smell was of bacon and eggs frying in the kitchen. My mother always had the house warm and breakfast ready no matter how early anybody in the family got up. She was so thoughtful and self-sacrificing that we were be-

2

ginning to get a little worried about her. She had few interests outside of my father, my brother, and me, and when she wasn't cooking or cleaning up after us she was doing the laundry, shoveling coal, or taking out the ashes. Fighting the furnace was rough work, but she seemed to be the only one with enough strength of character to do it, especially in the winter when it took a superhuman effort of the will to get out of bed at all.

We still had a coal furnace when everybody we knew had an oil burner, because my father thought oil heat smelled funny. He had several ideas like that, even though he read the *Dubuque Telegraph Herald* and the *Des Moines Register* every day and should have known better. He thought refrigerators gave food an "electric" taste, so mom was stuck with an icebox until the last firm in town that made ice went out of business. We didn't get an oil burner until the coal company quit making deliveries except to foundries and power plants.

Because of what mom had to put up with, I had written a letter several months earlier proposing her for sainthood and had given it to Sister Don Bosco to forward to the Pope. I was hoping for a favorable reply in time for mom's birthday. What a present that would make! How proud she would be! Unfortunately, there was a war on, and my letter may not have gotten through. It was the fall of 1943, and although the Allies were getting closer the Vatican was still in the hands of the Italians.

Rising above the towering elms that lined both sides of the street was the high, peaked roof of our two-story house, which had been built before I was born by my father and my Uncle Ed. They wanted the house to be the most imposing in the neighborhood, and they wanted it to last. The roof carried handsome slate shingles, and the basement walls were made of heavy, quarried limestone. Front and back were broad, screened-in porches where we sometimes ate when the inside of the house was too hot. All of the porch furniture seemed to move in some way. There were a variety of antique rocking chairs, a wide swing attached to the ceiling by two chains, and a glider whose squeaks nobody could stand for more than ten seconds. Even the big table on the back porch was on casters, which meant that you couldn't put your elbows on it during meals.

As I went out the front door that morning I saw mom take her place under the blue silk star that hung in the front window. She found time every day to sit there and say a rosary for Paul. It was working, too, because after a year of combat he still hadn't suffered so much as a scratch.

It was hard to feel threatened by the war when you were in a place as remote from the action as Iowa. North America stretched for so many thousands of miles in all directions that there wasn't an enemy plane in existence that could have reached us. Nevertheless, I had a plan of action worked out in case a Messerschmitt roared out of the sun on a strafing run. As the bullets kicked up a path along the ground toward me, I would jump behind a tree and throw a clod of dirt as high as I could, hitting the pilot in the eyes and making the plane crash in a ball of yellow flame followed by a civic reception in my honor at the Hotel Julien.

A bombardier would have found in Dubuque very little to engage his interest, but that doesn't mean it was nothing but a hick town. It had a population of thirty thousand and boasted a formidable meat-packing plant, a large sash and door company, and a factory that made nationally known plumbing fittings. At Dyersville, twenty-five miles away, was a church that had been designated a Basilica, which meant that the Pope would set up shop there if he were ever in the vicinity. As a matter of fact, there were so many seminaries, convents, churches, monasteries, and Catholic schools in the Greater Dubuque Area that it could have served nicely as world headquarters for the hierarchy had the fascists decided to occupy the Vatican and turn it into a fort or a restaurant.

But there is no denying that agriculture was one of the main reasons for the existence of the town—which was obvious on Saturdays, when farmers from places like Epworth, Peosta, and Zwingle came in to do their shopping. Their bib overalls, freshly laundered for the city visit, and their tanned faces made them conspicuous among the pedestrians downtown. Watching other people was one of their chief entertainments, and on summer weekends at least half of the cars parked along Main Street were filled with farm families, faces at the windows. They also enjoyed parking along the banks of the Mississippi and watching the silent flow of the brown water. The appearance of a tugboat pushing a string of barges was an event to be talked about for weeks. There was little else to do. At night there were baseball games, but the ball park was on a bottom land where mists from the river mingled with smoke from freight trains to make the outfielders all but invisible.

The hills and bluffs that lined the river drew back from the western bank to make room for Dubuque. From Eagle Point Park or from any of a dozen other high places you could almost see the whole of it—the dark, steel bridges to Illinois and Wisconsin, the church steeples poking through the trees, the brick buildings in the business district, and the mansions of the rich perched like prison watchtowers on the brows of the green hills. Under a blanket of snow in the winter and a blanket of heat in the summer the town gave the impression of waiting for something.

It was a better place for kids than grownups. The snow, the hills, the steep streets—especially the steep streets—were little more than inconveniences to adults. But to kids they offered endless recreational possibilities, most of which involved speed. Certain of my grade-school friends I can remember only as streaking past my house on scooters, roller skates, bicycles, sleds, skis, toboggans, or ice skates. Ice skates weren't confined to the frozen harbor; after a sleet storm they could be used anywhere.

3

Hank Clancy was about halfway through the twenty buttons on the front of his black cassock when I came into the altar boys' dressing room at the rear of St. Procopius Church. He looked at me with alarm.

"What the hell are you doing here?"

"I'm going to serve with you," I said.

"What about Mule?"

"Mule's sick."

"Oh, Jesus, no," he groaned, and stopped buttoning.

I hunted through the rack of cassocks until I found one about the right length.

Hank closed his eyes and sank to a bench. "Oh, Jesus, no," he said again.

"Don't worry, Hank, I can do it. I've been serving in the nuns' chapel."

His eyes popped open. "But you've never served a High Mass, have you? Have you?"

"Well, not exactly, but I've been practicing at noon with Sister Conceptus."

"Oh, Jesus, no." He began buttoning, grimly. Suddenly he pointed a finger at me. "Look, if we get into trouble out there, just get on your goddam knees and stay there, will you? And don't make any responses unless you know goddam well what to say."

"*Ad Deum qui laetificat juventutem meam,*" I said, to show him I knew my responses as well as the next guy. We slipped our starched white surplices over our heads. "*Suscipiat Dominus sacrificium,*" I went on, "*de manibus tuis, ad laudem et gloriam nominis sui, ad utilitatem quoque nostrum, totiusque Ecclesiae. . . .*"

"Oh, shut up," said Hank.

He had good reason to be uneasy about having to serve Mass with me. For one thing the difference in our sizes was going to make us both look a little ridiculous. He was a senior in high school, a tackle on the football team, and was both tall and broad. I wasn't short for my age but I was only thirteen and very thin, so thin that my father said I could have a fist fight through a keyhole. When two altar boys served Mass a lot of symmetrical movements were called for—when one walked, hands folded prayerfully, to one side of the altar, the other walked at the same speed to the other side in order to keep the scene in balance. When they returned to the center they genuflected in unison and bowed to each other. It was a sort of low-grade ballet, not without comical overtones.

Another thing that no doubt worried Hank was that I was one of the new breed of altar boys being trained by Sister Conceptus, who was obsessed with such basics as the proper enunciation of Church Latin. She had the unorthodox idea that worshipers in the rear pews should be able to hear every word, and she drilled us on speaking loudly and with exaggerated distinctness. Father Grundy was going to rue the day he approved her as head of altar boys, because with the grenadiers she was turning out Mass would take at least twenty minutes longer.

Sister Conceptus was a nun, but she had no intention of staying in the background and letting the priests have it all their way. She meant to climb to the top of her profession, and you didn't do that by sneaking around like a mouse. If she was to be in charge of altar boys, then, by God, she'd make them the best in the business. She was going to make it to Mother Superior or know the reason why.

Hank lit all the candles on the altar, not trusting any of them to me, and when he returned to the sacristy we stood together while Father went through the ritual of putting on his vestments and draping various pieces of embroidered cloth over the chalice.

"That's the alb," I pointed out to Hank in a whisper to let him know that I was solidly grounded in the fundamentals. "That's the chasuble. The prayer he's saying now means 'Gird me, O Lord, with the cincture of purity and extinguish in my heart the fire of concupiscence.' "

Hank ignored me, but I knew he couldn't help being impressed.

By peeking around a large vase of flowers I saw that the church was practically full—at least two hundred and fifty men, women, and children were sitting in the smooth, wooden pews waiting for Mass to begin. More were coming in all the time, blessing themselves with holy water as they came down the aisles and genuflecting before taking their seats. It was a big turnout for a weekday morning. In the balcony at the rear stood Sister Mary Valeriamina, who had a degree in music, with her Upperclass Mixed Choir of juniors and seniors, each holding a hymnal. Mrs. Hofstaeder, watching in her little mirror for our appearance in the sanctuary, sat hunched over the keyboard of the mighty St. Procopius pipe organ, whose giant pipes lined the loft. To the naturally musty odor of the old church was added the smell of burning candles and incense.

I began to feel a little nervous. The nuns' chapel I was used to was hardly bigger than our parlor at home and Sister Conceptus could prompt me from the front row. But that was all behind me. I was in the big time now and on my own.

4

When Father Grundy was ready he turned around, holding the covered chalice in front of his heart, and nodded for us to go. He was an old man with wispy hair and indistinct features, and it was hard to imagine him ever having been plagued by the fire of concupiscence.

Hank and I marched side by side through the archway into the sanctuary between the altar and the communion railing. Father, head bowed, was close behind. The moment we appeared Mrs. Hofstaeder brought her hands and feet crashing down on the keys and pedals of the organ. The deafening burst of sound nearly gave everybody a heart attack—it was ten times louder than the roar made by the three P-38's that once buzzed the playground. The whole church quivered down to its foundations, the stained-glass windows rattled, and several people in the congregation gasped in fright. Even Mrs. Hofstaeder was surprised and admitted later that the volume was a bit excessive even for the Twelfth Thursday Before the Epiphany.

Hank, a seasoned campaigner, plunged forward as if nothing had happened, but I was so startled by the concussion that I froze in my tracks. Father Grundy ran into me from behind and almost knocked me down, the chalice hitting me in the back of the head. I whirled around with the terrible expectation of seeing the chalice and the paten and the burse and wafers and the whole works scattered all over the floor, but Father had managed to hang on and things were only disarranged slightly. He went back into the sacristy to make sure nothing was missing and drape the veil evenly over the chalice again. I followed him, whispering apologies.

"I'm *sorry*, Father, I'm *sorry*. The organ—it scared me. . . ."

"Have you ever served Mass before?" he asked in a low, even voice, not looking at me, striving to avoid the sin of Passion.

"Oh, yes, Father. This was just an accident."

"All right. We won't speak of it again."

Hank in the meantime had walked all the way to the foot of the altar. He genuflected, turned and bowed to where he thought I would be standing bowing back to him. When he saw that he was alone, he looked back and forth in confusion. The congregation, which had risen to its feet, was also puzzled, and some of the people were sitting down again. Mrs. Hofstaeder, unable to find us anywhere in her mirror, was easing the pressure, allowing the music to trail off uncertainly. We waited for Hank, who was blushing deeply, to return to the sacristy.

A few minutes later we marched into view again, this time holding our formation in good order. At the center of the altar we genuflected like synchronized swimmers. As Father mounted the four steps to the top of the platform, Hank and I bowed to each other and knelt on the bottom step as symmetrically as our contrasting physiques would allow. Mrs. Hofstaeder took it again from the beginning and held the volume of her powerful instrument within acceptable limits. The Holy Sacrifice of the Mass was proceeding with its customary stateliness and gravity.

5

St. Procopius was a very large church. I had seen pictures of cathedrals like Chartres and Notre Dame, and they didn't seem much larger.

St. Procopius didn't have flying buttresses, but it did have a couple of imposing plaster columns inside supporting a high vaulted ceiling festooned with religious paintings. Wherever you looked there were rich details to examine. On the side walls were tall, stained-glass windows, each one portraying a saint, and between them were bas-reliefs of the Stations of the Cross. Behind the altar was an enormous wooden backdrop composed of gilded ornamentation, scroll work, and niches for flowers, candles, and statues. At the very top, fully thirty feet above the altar, was a massive crucifix, to which was nailed a shockingly realistic, larger-than-life Christ. His knees were buckled to show that most of His weight was hanging from the nails driven through the palms of His hands. His head was hanging to one side, and because He was gazing heavenward you could see most of the whites of His eyes. A crown of thorns caused rivulets of blood to course down His pale cheeks and chest. Blood also oozed from the nail wounds in His hands and feet and from the slit in His side where He had been lanced by a sadistic Italian soldier.

All in all He was in extremely poor condition. I don't know if He was supposed to be dead already or not. If He wasn't dead, He was certainly moribund, and having Him hanging there injected a note of deep melancholy into the atmosphere.

The old church and its decorations were conducive to daydreaming. You were supposed to concentrate on the Mass, but that was difficult because it hardly ever varied. The same old thing, day after day, century after century. Adding to the dullness was that it was said in Latin, a language people seldom spoke even in Rome.

There wasn't much to do at Mass unless you were a priest, altar boy, or member of the choir—nothing to say and nothing to sing. All the congregation had to do was stand, sit, and kneel at the right times and have some loose change ready for the collection basket. I wasn't the only one who spent a lot of time daydreaming. My mother, who never took her eyes out of her missal during Mass, always had her week's shopping planned by the time she left the church. People who didn't use missals, like my father, spent quite a bit of time studying the geometric patterns in the ceiling and windows. Dad was a concrete contractor. I know that he sometimes thought about his work because one Sunday as we were walking to our car after Mass he announced that he had finally calculated what he was going to bid on the Langworthy Avenue curb and gutter job.

6

My daydreams were of a different sort. I usually stared at a certain circular stained-glass window that was made up of a series of swirls and curves—curves that reminded me of Gretchen Schwartz's boobs. Now it may be asked how I knew what Gretchen Schwartz's boobs looked like, since she always kept them well hidden and would never have shown them to me, a mere eighth-grader. But the fact is I had once been face to face with them at point-blank range. She didn't know it, though. She would have died had she known it. For the record, I saw Gretchen Schwartz naked at twenty-five minutes after five on the morning of February 2, 1943. It was pitch dark except for a distant streetlight, and I was crunching through the snow in my galoshes, overcoat, mittens, stocking cap, and earmuffs on my way to the goddam nuns' chapel. The air was very cold and my breath made white puffs in front of me. Her house had once been a grocery store and was close to the sidewalk. The light was on in the front window as I walked past, and although the shade was drawn there was a rip in it and a small triangular piece was hanging down at eye level. Naturally I paused and peered through the opening. That's when I saw Gretchen Schwartz walk out of the bathroom without any clothes on. The light was bright, and she was no more than six feet away, completely open for inspection. She stood looking around on the floor for something, with her boobs staring straight at me. I stared back in astonishment, trying to comprehend the great good luck that had come my way and already fearing that my friends would never believe it. I swept my eyes up and down her body like a paint brush, striving frantically to commit every detail to memory. When she bent over to pick up her panties, her boobs drew away from her body in a way that gave me an almost instantaneous erection and burned a tableau into my mind that has stayed vividly with me down through the years. Open-mouthed and wide-eyed I watched her wiggle into her panties and deftly smother her boobs in the twin snoods of a brassiere. What happened next I can't say because the glass became fogged with my breath, and I was afraid she would hear the squeaking if I tried to wipe it clear.

I turned away from the window and staggered off through the snow and darkness, leaving a drunken trail of footprints. I had to walk stiff-leggedly to avoid hurting myself because my erection was straining painfully against my shorts and pushing my clothes outward like a tent-pole. Had I walked into a tree or a wall I would have been killed instantly. That erection stayed with me for at least thirty minutes—I know it lasted through the Introit and well into the Kyrie.

From that morning on, the mere sight of Gretchen Schwartz—even the sight of her house—stimulated a rising in my loins. An odd thing about it was that she was not an erotic object to anybody else. She had acne, her front teeth stuck out, and she appeared to be shapeless. But she and I knew how sexily she was built—other people went on being fooled by the loose clothes that concealed her ins and outs.

CHAPTER TWO

1

My daydreams about Gretchen were swept away when I realized Father Grundy and Hank had begun exchanging Latin phrases without warning. They went so fast that I had to flip several pages in my missal to find the place. Father said only the first word plainly, as a clue, then ran the rest of the sentence together in a low hum. Hank's responses were barely audible buzzes. I tensed myself and got ready to jump in.

"*Gloria hmmm hmmm,*" Father Grundy said.

"*Bzz bzz,*" Hank replied, while at the same time I said in a clear voice: "*Sicut erat in principio, et nunc, et semper: et in saecula saeculorum.*" I enunciated each syllable distinctly, as God intended. If Sister Conceptus was in the church I knew she would be proud. She might even paste a blue star after my name in her book. Five blue stars meant a gold star trimmed in white, and five gold stars brought a scapular medal blessed by the bishop.

Hank didn't appreciate my instrusion into what

he apparently felt was a private conversation between him and Father Grundy. He looked at me as if I were throwing some kind of fit. Father hesitated for a moment and then said, "*Introibo hmm hmm.*" Before Hank could buzz anything in return I cut in brightly with "*Ad Deum qui laetificat juventutem meam.*" My rendering of these words was a model of clarity, and the stir I heard in the congregation I took to be an expression of approval. I must have been the first of Sister Conceptus's shock troops that they had heard.

Father Grundy expressed no approval though. He seemed suddenly weak, and he took hold of the edge of the altar table for support. When he recovered he cast a pained glance at Hank, mouthing something I didn't catch and nodding toward me. Whatever the message was, Hank caught it. He leaned sideways with a ferocious expression on his face and hissed in my ear: "Cut that shit out or we'll be in here all day."

I cut that shit out. I knelt in silence while they traded *bzzs* and *hmms*, too afraid of Hank to open my mouth. Sister Conceptus would raise hell with me later for giving up so easily. "Well, Thomas," she would say, "we didn't show much stick-to-itiveness this morning, did we?" But she didn't see the look on Hank's face, a look that carried a promise of violence.

For the next five or ten minutes I was like a zombie. The color had left my face and my eyes were glassy. I made no further effort for the time being to take part in the Holy Sacrifice of the Mass, except to stand up and kneel down when I had to. I wasn't worried about Sister Conceptus. She could impugn my stick-to-itiveness all she wanted to and even slap me around a little to add drama to her altar boy class. I could survive that. What worried me was what Hank was going to do when he got me alone. But before long I was too occupied with problems at hand to think about the future.

2

With a beatific expression on his square face, Hank walked past me carrying the paten, a small, gold dish. Without warning he slammed it into my stomach as hard as he could. "Communion time, stupid," he said.

I took the paten in one hand and rubbed my stomach with the other, sneering contemptuously at him as if it didn't hurt at all. I knew why he wanted me to serve communion; he thought I would make a fool of myself. Father Grundy was the fastest communion-giver in the world, and to keep up with him the altar boy had to have terrific coordination. The people receiving knelt at the communion rail, and with quick sidesteps the old priest faced each one in turn, slipping a Host into their mouths almost before they could get them open and their tongues out. With each blurred movement of his hand away from the chalice, in which the little white discs were piled like rolls of quarters, the altar boy had to make a fencer's lunge with the paten to get it under the communicant's chin before the Host reached his tongue. It took nice timing on everybody's part, and when properly done it reminded me of the mechanical bottle cappers at the Dubuque Star brewery.

Everybody wanted to know what a Host looked like up close, but there was no way to find out. Pretending to swallow it but actually keeping it in your mouth with the idea of examining it later was absolutely the worst thing you could do. Sister Raphael told us what happened to one of her pupils who tried it. He sneaked behind a parked car after Mass and spit the thin, round cracker into his hand. Right away blood gushed out of his mouth and splashed on the street and it didn't stop until he put it back in. His clothes got drenched with blood and he very nearly died. The street looked as if someone had butchered a hog. A group of scientists examined him later, but with their shallow, materialistic viewpoints they couldn't even begin to understand what had happened.

Some of the kids laughed at this story and said it wasn't true, but nobody could bring himself to test it. Except Wanda Farney's big brother. They say he took a Host out of his mouth once and nothing happened to him, even when he flushed it down a toilet in the Illinois Central depot. We couldn't ask him about it, though, because he was in the Quartermaster Corps in Libya.

Helping the priest during communion gave you a pretty good look at the Host, and I could have told everybody that it didn't look like the Body of

Christ, although it was. Father Grundy explained this seeming contradiction to us in religion class after he heard that some of the first- and second-graders thought that the Hosts were really little pieces of meat and that the wine, which only the priest drinks at Mass, was really blood, which actually it is, odd though that may sound to untrained ears. As he explained, before the Consecration the Hosts are just wafers of unleavened bread and the wine is simply wine. But during the Consecration they are changed into the actual Body and Blood of Christ, remaining bread and wine in *appearance* only. By any so-called scientific test that puny Man could make they would *seem* to be what they were before, but they *really* and in fact *were* the Body and Blood of Christ, miraculously transformed by the direct intervention of God the Father during the Mass, which therefore in a real and physical sense is a reenactment of the Last Supper, during which Christ took some unleavened bread and said, "Take ye all and eat of this, for this is My Body!" and took some wine and said, "Take ye all and drink of this, for this is the chalice of My blood of the new and eternal covenant, the mystery of faith, which shall be shed for you and many unto the forgiveness of sins." This is hard to explain to children in the lower grades.

If Hank Clancy thought I was going to be unable to keep up with Father Grundy during the
dispensing of communion he was going to be disappointed, for I intended to perform flawlessly.
My cassock was a trifle too long and I nearly
stumbled over it a couple of times at first, but I
quickly learned the trick of lifting it slightly
above my shoes with my free hand. The required
pious expression was no problem; I had perfected
that years ago. I was naturally pale, and when I
lifted my eyebrows and half closed my eyes anybody would have sworn that I was in an extreme
state of grace, which was true on occasion. The
hardest part for me was to control my thoughts,
which were often more lurid than I care to describe.

A lot of other people had very good pious expressions, too, and I often wondered if behind
those masks their thoughts were as sensational as
mine. I knew that some of the saintliest-looking
ones weren't saintly at all. Like Helene Hanson.
She had luxurious, pointed tits and she always
had them jacked up like a pair of antiaircraft
guns. She must have known that she was keeping
the toilet stalls of St. Procopius full of boys ma-
nipulating themselves. Self-abuse, as you can well
imagine, was a sin. Yet she had the gall to mince
her way to the communion rail with a look on her
face of utter innocence. When Father Grundy

and I came to her, I had all I could do to keep from rapping her on the neck with the paten. She couldn't possibly have been in a state of grace with her tits aiming at us like that.

But I fought against such lines of thought and tried to keep my mind on liturgical matters. The trouble was that I knew almost everybody who was receiving, and each one reminded me of something.

Who could see Mr. and Mrs. Walsh without thinking of the Hawaiian luau they tried to give one Christmas Eve? They gave a lot of parties, even though there was a war on, as did all the other rich people who lived on Fremont Avenue, played golf, and bought their clothes in Chicago. Mr. Walsh bought a whole pig from the meat-packing company and buried it in the back yard in a pit filled with hot coals. Several hours later, when it was time to eat, night had fallen, along with several inches of snow. They couldn't find the pit, much less the pig. They looked for a long time with flashlights and shovels before giving up and driving to East Dubuque with their guests for chop suey at the Green Pagoda. They found the pig during the spring thaw, but very little of it was usable.

Old lady Foley was there at the rail, as usual. She received communion seven days a week. My Uncle Ed claimed that she sometimes went to Mass at several churches on the same day and received at every one. Doing that wasn't forbidden by canon law, but it certainly was redundant. Once you had partaken of the Holy Eucharist there was nothing further you could do because your soul was already spotlessly pure. A speeding truck could be faced serenely, because your soul would ascend directly to heaven if it became separated from your body. There was no way to buy flight insurance or whatever it was she was trying to do.

4

You can tell a lot about people by the way they stick out their tongues. For instance, Pat Kenneally, the policeman, opened his mouth and thrust his big flat tongue out boldly, fearing nothing—but he didn't close his eyes the way he was supposed to. Mrs. Walsh stuck hers out just a little way, feeling foolish about it. Helene Hanson let her tongue slide slowly into view, as if rehearsing a French kiss.

I wondered what holy Mrs. Foley, as we called her, would do, because she always kept her lips pursed and her nose wrinkled. Even when she smiled she never showed more than two or three teeth. She knelt at the rail with her hands folded at her chest and her head bowed so low that her chin was on her knuckles. When we got to her she tilted her head back, formed a small hole with her lips, and then blocked it with the tip of her tongue. Apparently it was the best she could do—she must have had a condition. Father Grundy didn't hesitate a second. He wedged a wafer between her tongue and upper lip and

24

pushed it home with his thumb as if forcing a coin into a jammed candy machine.

Officer Kenneally, in contrast, presented an easy target, but it was odd serving communion to a man wearing a gun. Nobody minded that he went to Mass while on duty or that he parked his squad car in front of the hydrant, but a lot of people didn't feel it was right for him to wear his gun. No word was ever said to him about it, though, because he was a very touchy person. He had a battered nose and a square jaw and he patterned himself after Captain Easy in the comic strip *Wash Tubbs*. Sometimes, according to his younger brother Roger, he sat up in bed in the middle of the night and shouted sentences from recent episodes.

Pat's gun wasn't just an ornament—it was a working tool of his trade and he used it frequently, if inaccurately. One night the dispatcher at the railroad yard called the cops to report a drunk sleeping in a boxcar at the foot of Third Street. Pat Kenneally showed up with his siren screaming. He screeched to a stop, jumped out, and fired all of his bullets into the darkness. Fortunately, the drunk had heard him coming and had gotten the hell out. The slugs didn't do anything but break some windows in a caboose parked on the next track. A few days later the railroad hired some guards of its own.

Pat's police officer's cap, whistle, and blue coat were borrowed on another night for a prank that made his young brother one of the best-liked kids in school. Roger put them on and with piercing blasts on the whistle blocked traffic on Dodge Street, which was U.S. Highway 30. He simply stood in the middle of the street with his hand raised, stopping all the cars. After about five minutes there were fifteen or twenty lined up in each direction. Some of the drivers at the head of the lines, not able to see any reason for the delay, decided to get out and ask the short cop with the long coat what the trouble was. As soon as they opened their doors Roger turned and in a very unpolicemanlike manner ran as fast as he could between two houses and disappeared into a storm sewer.

5

Having somebody at the communion railing wearing a gun was nothing compared to somebody wearing nothing at all. It was just my luck that Gretchen Schwartz was receiving that morning. I knew I was going to be in trouble when I saw her kneeling there without a stitch on—which was how she always appeared to me. She made it easy for Father Grundy; she opened her mouth and put her tongue well out. Her buck teeth seemed to swing outward helpfully, like saloon doors. Holding the paten, my hand was only inches from the outline of the breasts I knew and loved so well, and immediately I was aware of a familiar hardening inside my fly. If she didn't have such a homely face and if there hadn't been several hundred people around, I think I would have tried to lie down on her right then and there.

But what a time to get an erection! I had to get rid of it, but how? I remembered a method taught to me by Brother Bartholomew, a frail, old Trappist monk from the monastery outside of town who had once lectured the boys in the school—one at a time, privately—on how to quash the temptations of the flesh and avoid the sins of lust, libidinousness, and filthy thoughts. His formula was simple: Think about sports. I don't know if it worked for him—he didn't seem athletically inclined—but it often worked for me.

I forced myself to recall the time I beat a meter reader out of eighty-five cents on the pool table in our basement; I thought of how wonderful it would be when the war was over and Mickey Marty was back in the Loras College Fieldhouse banking in hook shots right- and left-handed; I thought of Doc Blanchard smashing the middle and Glenn Davis sweeping wide. But it didn't work. Ten people past Gretchen, and I was still in a gross state of masculinity. Communicants knowing where to look would have noticed an inappropriate lump in my cassock.

In God's own house I had a hard-on! During communion! The magnitude of the sin I was committing scared me, and I thought of the extra pain I was causing my Blessed Saviour, hanging on a cross behind me. I prayed fervently to Him and to St. Joseph for help—it didn't seem right to pray to the Blessed Virgin. I pressed forward gamely with my paten, struggling to maintain a sanctimonious look on my face even though pain

27

and tears could be seen there as I begged Our
Lord for assistance and forgiveness. I had a wild
vision of Sister Conceptus or, worse yet, Sister
Raphael, running to the front of the church
pointing at my crotch, shouting, "Thomas! What
is the meaning of this?"

I had heard that nurses had a way of making a
rigid dork collapse like a flat tire by flicking it
with their fingers or striking it crisply with the
edges of their hands, but I didn't know exactly
how they did it or whether it would work through
a cassock. As my panic grew I began to repeat to
myself the Latin that Father recited as he placed
the Host on each tongue: "*Corpus Domine nostri
Jesu Christi custodiat animam tuam in vitam ae-
ternam.* Amen." I hoped that endlessly repeating
a sentence from the magic language of Holy
Mother Church would somehow make my flesh
subside. I meant to whisper the words so that Father Grundy wouldn't think I was trying to cor-
rect him in front of everybody, but in my ner-
vousness I started to speak out loud. Father gave
me a severe look. "Shh!" he hissed.

That did it. The pressure in my pants began to
drop. The humiliation of being publicly rebuked
coupled with the fear of divine retribution spiked
my desire, and my rigidity gradually ebbed away.
I breathed in relief as drops of cold sweat ran
down my sides.

When Communion was over and I was kneeling once more at the foot of the altar, I looked up
at my Blessed Saviour, half expecting to see His
divine countenance suffused in a warm glow of

appreciation for the effort I had made to avoid offending Him. But He didn't seem to be paying attention. He still was in a very desperate condition medically.

Had there been the slightest change in His expression, of course, we would have had a miracle on our hands. That wouldn't have been too much to ask, in my opinion. I was always disappointed when nothing supernatural happened at logical times. It seemed to me that in view of all the fasting and penances and kneeling and dogma that we had to contend with as Catholics, God should have worked some kind of a miracle once in a while to show us that we were at least on the right track. There were occasional inner feelings of conviction and purity and things like that, but nothing *solid* ever happened that you could really get your hands on. I wanted an obvious sign. I didn't want my life to be one long test of faith.

Holy Mrs. Foley claimed that she was lighting a vigil candle in front of the statue of the Blessed Virgin on December 7, 1941, and saw a tear fall from the sorrowful plaster eye at the very instant Japanese bombs hit the battleship *Arizona*, but you can believe that or not, as you like. We asked Father Grundy about it, and he gave us a very roundabout answer before finally admitting that believing what Mrs. Foley said was not essential for salvation.

6

At the side of the altar I gave Hank a smile and tried to insinuate myself into his good graces. We were filling the glass cruets with water that the priest would pour over his consecrated fingers during the Lavabo.

"I guess I'll be seeing you tonight out on the golf course," I whispered.

He didn't answer.

"Porky lights a fart tonight," I reminded him.

"So what has that got to do with you? He'll never let a punk like you watch."

"Like hell he won't. You just wait and see. I've been. . . ."

"Will you shut up, for chrissakes? Don't you know there's a Mass on?"

He made me mad, the big bastard. If only night would come! Then we would see who was a punk and who was not.

I was still mad five minutes later when I tripped over the bell. I was on my way from the Gospel side to the Epistle side with the altar missal, which was not only heavy but was so big that I couldn't see where I was stepping. Genuflecting with such a weight sent burning pains through my thighs, but I had to pretend that it was light as a feather. The small silver bell was kept on the bottom step when not in use—it was the altar boys' job to pick it up and give it a jingle several times during Mass when the people were supposed to

fall on their knees or strike their breasts symboli-
cally with their fists. The bell at St. Procopius
had a very harsh and piercing tone, and to the
daydreamers it could be as startling as a telephone ringing in the middle of the night. The bell
at Holy Ghost, on the other hand, was soft and
mellow, which may have been because the pastor
at Holy Ghost was fat Father Pusateri, who was
soft and mellow, too.

I was coming down the altar steps with the
missal, thinking about God only knows what,
when I stepped right on the bell, sending it ringing across the floor. I lost my balance and had
the sickening knowledge that the missal was falling forward out of my control. I took several wild
steps to get under it, and I might have made it if I
hadn't tripped over the hem of my cassock. When
that happened I went down just as dramatically
as if my feet had been knocked out from under
me. With a stunning thud I landed full length on
the floor. My face ended up inches from the bell
and for some crazy reason I got the idea that it
was vital to get it back where it belonged, so I
grabbed it and flipped it over to Hank as if it
were a live grenade. He was taken by complete
surprise. The bell hit him on the chest and he
slapped at it down the front of his body trying to
get hold of it. It was ringing furiously and people
were kneeling down and striking their breasts all
over the place.

I scrambled to my feet, scooped up the missal,
and hustled up the altar steps on the Epistle side,
giving Hank a wide berth in case he made a lunge

for me. I put the missal on the table quickly, trying not to notice the corners of ripped pages that were sticking out here and there. I was in for it now.

Dear God, I prayed, forgive me, for I knew not what I did and I didn't do it on purpose. I had a notion to bolt from the church and hop a freight by Julien Dubuque's grave, but where would I go? How would I get in touch with other excommunicated people? What would life be like with defrocked priests, disgraced nuns, and perverted unbelievers? How far would I get in a cassock and surplice?

Father Grundy grabbed my wrist and squeezed it hard. "What's the matter with you?" he demanded, trying to keep his voice down to a whisper.

I stared at the floor desolately.

He released me and pointed to a corner of the sanctuary. "Kneel down over there," he said, "and don't move until I tell you to."

"Yes, Father." I slunk to the corner and dropped to my knees.

7

I took out my beads and began silently saying a rosary for each of the Five Sorrowful Mysteries—The Agony of Jesus, The Scourging, The Crowning with Thorns. The Carrying of the Cross, and The Crucifixion. Halfway through the first Hail Mary I noticed that Hank's face had gone strangely dark. He was kneeling at the foot of the altar, staring at me with wild eyes and flaring nostrils. Every few seconds he leaned toward me, obviously having trouble restraining himself from leaping to his feet for a physical attack.

What was eating him? It occurred to me then that by flipping him the bell I had made him look ridiculous in front of the whole congregation. When I was on the floor I was out of sight behind the rail. What most people saw was Hank Clancy slapping at the bell on his chest and legs as if trying to kill a moth. The ringing of the bell had thoroughly confused the congregation; Elbows Hilken told me later that he and his whole family had gotten up and walked out, thinking there was a fire drill.

Without my realizing it, a smile crept across my face, and a moment later I heard a horrible sound—my own laughter. I cut it off instantly, of course, but not before Father Grundy looked at me as if I were the hunchback of Notre Dame. I began coughing strenuously, trying to make him believe that I was having some sort of allergic attack. Laughing during the Benedicamus! Jesus Christ, I hated to think what he would do to me for that. I couldn't meet his gaze, and to go on fingering my beads seemed suddenly foolish, so I dropped them and opened my missal, staring at it unseeingly until Mass was over.

I got into the sacristy a few steps ahead of Father and Hank. The people in the pews were filing into the aisles while the voices of the choir and the organ climbed to their final crescendos.

As soon as I was out of sight of the congregation I turned and ran into the passageway behind the altar. I had no intention of hanging around and letting both Father and Hank jump on me at once. Later in the day would be soon enough, after they had cooled down a little. Down the steps to the dressing room I flew, unbuttoning my cassock and pulling my surplice over my head as I went. . . .

There was only one place within reach where I would be safe—the pile of screens in the Band Room. I raced across the alley alongside the church and into the playground behind the school. Up the fire escape I went, taking the steps two and three at a time to the top landing. I swung my legs over the railing onto a foot-wide gutter at the lower edge of the nearly vertical roof, forty feet above the ground. My back flattened against the shingles, I edged my way carefully to the first window, raising it with my fingers behind me. A moment later I was inside the Band Room and hidden in a small compartment several of us had built under a pile of screens that were stored there.

I could see out, but nobody could see in. It was like a burial crypt inside an Egyptian pyramid, and could be reached only by knowing which screen covered the entrance to the narrow crawl space. As far as the general public was concerned, I had vanished without a trace.

CHAPTER THREE

1

It was a wonderful secret room and I could have hidden there for months without detection. Only Roger Kenneally, Kites Callahan, and Elbows Hilken knew about it. We often sneaked in there to play cards and smoke during the confusion of pep rallies or all-school assemblies in the church basement. The hideout had an army blanket on the floor, a candle, a couple of half-eaten C-rations, and a Street and Smith adventure magazine with a color cover showing a wounded parachutist shooting a Tommy gun at a pack of wild dogs.

The Band Room was full of folding chairs, music stands, instruments, and shelves of music. It was the only room on the third floor that could be used by students, the others being given over to living quarters for the nuns, which had never been seen by anybody, except Roger, Kites, Elbows, and me. Once a year we tiptoed through the curtained doorway into Forbidden Territory when we knew nobody was there—during the

Homecoming Bonfire in the parking lot across the street. A pile of cardboard and trash fifteen feet high going up in flames was a spectacular sight against a dark sky, and the streets, sidewalks, and yards around the school were always filled with people watching it. As soon as the nuns filed through the front door of the school to stand on the lawn—where they could listen to the speeches and yells and get a good view of the fire—the four of us would push our way into the darkness on the third floor seeking danger and excitement, seeing things never seen before by students or alumni, and tasting the thrills normally enjoyed only by burglars.

The most interesting things we discovered on those risky explorations were the bathrooms. For some reason it was fascinating to look at the toilets the nuns used. None of us could imagine a nun sitting on a toilet, certainly not Sister Raphael or Sister Conceptus. It was like trying to picture a saint or an angel in such a position. We knew nuns were people, but there was something weird and unearthly about them and it was odd to think of them having to concern themselves with natural functions of the body. We snickered and giggled, but I, for one, felt that I had a deeper understanding of the various religious orders because I had seen those toilets. They brought home to me in a vivid way the realization that those who answered God's call and gave up their lives to work in His service were not relieved by Him of their fleshly burdens and desires, as one might suppose.

The fact that nuns were largely human was concealed by the way they dressed. The only parts of them you could see were their hands and faces. The rest, from head to foot, was covered by black cloth, except for a piece of starched white fabric that covered their chests like a triangular dart board, and another piece of stiff white cardboard that grew out of their foreheads like a misplaced French cuff. Their necks and the sides of their heads were wrapped in bandages, so you couldn't see their ears or their hair. They may not have had any hair. The rumor was that when they took their vows they accepted a lifetime of GI haircuts to make it impossible to commit the sin of Vanity.

Wondering what their heads looked like under the veils, bandages, and cardboard kept our minds busy all through grade school. Wanda Farney once stepped on a nun's veil on the stairs by accident and yanked the whole apparatus off the top of her head, but Wanda was so shaken by the incident that she couldn't describe what she had seen—either that or she had been sworn to secrecy. Most of the girls had big sucks with the nuns and were always on their side.

A nun on the move, veils and skirts streaming in her wake, was an impressive spectacle, not only to see but to hear. Once when sneaking around on the third floor during the bonfire, I lagged behind the others and found myself standing at one end of a dark corridor when a speeding nun entered the other. I couldn't tell which nun it was because in silhouette they tended toward sameness. Trapped, I climbed into the janitor's trash can and doubled up at the bottom, hoping to be mistaken for a pile of rags. The sound of her long strides as she approached was unnerving, to say the least. I heard the swish-swish of her habit, the rattle of the long string of beads hanging from her black leather belt, the click-click-click of the metal crucifix bouncing against her starched breastplate. Worst of all was the thump of her shoes as she came down the hall toward me. I closed my eyes and hugged my knees, listening to the approach of the pounding footsteps, which seemed to make the whole building shake. It must have been Sister Mary Clement, who weighed a ton.

When she got to the can she reached into it and began banging something against the side, setting up a terrific racket and scaring me half out of my wits. Did she think I was the Devil and was she trying to exorcise me as they did in the Dark Ages by beating on washtubs and drums? I hung on for dear life while a rain of fluffy crumbs and fine dust settled onto my head and neck. Then she stopped abruptly and retreated to the other end of the hallway, where she disappeared around a remote corner. I stayed frozen for at least five minutes before slowly raising my head.

Outside under a streetlight I figured out what had happened by examining the stuff that was down my neck and in my hair and ears. That damned Sister had emptied a pencil sharpener all over me! Jesus Christ! But I had a good time tell-

38

ing my friends about it. Years later I was still spinning tales about the time I was caught in a trash can by a huge nun who rolled it with me inside down three flights of stairs and across the playground to the dump.

2

After sitting in the screen room for a while I felt much better. What had I done that was so bad, really? I kicked the bell and fell on the floor with the missal, but I didn't do it maliciously. It could have happened to anybody. I couldn't help it if I had a coughing fit that sounded at first like laughter. So they get mad about it—what could they do? Brand me with a poker? Of course not. This wasn't medieval Spain; this was modern Iowa. If they laid a finger on me I'd squawk to every priest in the archbishopric.

I decided not to run away. Being a fugitive from your family, your church, and your school in peacetime was one thing, but during a war you had the armed forces to contend with.

My plan for the day was to stay out of trouble, take whatever penalties were dished out to me in the proper spirit of dumb acceptance, keep my mouth shut and my hands to myself, stay in line, and do what I was told. In short, be a good boy. I wanted nothing to crop up that would interfere with my being on time that night for the great fart lighting—or, as Kites Callahan called it, the annual dingleberry roast. Dingleberries, according to Kites, were the beads of dried fecal matter that hung on the hairs around the bunghole. I don't think he coined the term, but he used it a lot. Now that I think about him, he was always very much interested and amused by anything having to do with the lower alimentary canal. He once designed and made an army-style shoulder patch that depicted, he said, "an exploding fart on a field of dingleberries." He wanted everybody in the gang to wear it, but none of us ever did. Not that the idea wasn't good—it was just that he was a piss-poor artist.

Kites was a name we gave him because his ears stuck out. We used to tell him he would make an excellent commando because all you would have to do is throw him into the air and let him glide behind enemy lines.

When the warning bell rang for the start of the morning session, I walked casually down the stairs to the second floor and joined the stream of students. I greeted a couple of dozen of my friends and goosed Stanley Grant, bent over a bubbler, just as if I didn't have a care in the world. I couldn't see how being a nervous wreck would help any.

I kept my hands low and my eyes open to guard against anybody who might try to crump me. Crumping was a fad that had been popular with the older boys for a year or so and was still a constant threat. "To crump" was to use the back of your hand to hit somebody's balls. The object was not to incapacitate him, but merely to insult his dignity, and a flick of the hand was sufficient.

Even a light blow on the balls, however, could be painful and it paid to be vigilant, as you never knew when somebody might use a little too much force and be a little too accurate. The only good thing I can say about it is that it did tend to keep us all mentally alert and on our toes.

Porky walked by with a couple of his lieutenants as I stood by the eighth-grade door, and I gave him a wave and a hello. All I got in return, as usual, was a wink. That's the way he operated—no matter how conspicuously you greeted him he only winked, which was embarrassing sometimes because it looked as if you had been snubbed. His eyes darted from side to side, but he didn't turn his head, not because he was muscle-bound but because nobody was worth the effort. He was very muscular, though, and anyone trying to crump him would have been beaten to a pulp for his trouble. He walked with a measured tread, as if trying to wear out his shoes evenly. There were several guys bigger than Porky, but even they tried to stay on his good side; they knew how tough he was and how quick with his hands.

Naturally Father Amos, the football coach, drooled at the thought of Porky's speed and power harnessed in the service of St. Procopius on the gridiron, but Porky had little interest in sports. "If people want to fight they should fight," he said, "but not in sweat socks, knee pads, and jockstraps. That's all a lot of horseshit." One day, to Father Amos's delight and surprise, Porky showed up for football practice, which was held on the baked clay parking lot

41

across from the church. During the scrimmage Father Amos—sensing a championship for the St. Procopius Apostles in the Tri-State Catholic League—put Porky in as fullback with instructions to try a center plunge. Porky thought that was a stupid idea, so took off around end instead and, when big Mule Kahlbach, the team captain on defense, tried to bring him down with a flying tackle, Porky grabbed him by the chinstrap and flung him into the stickerbushes alongside the Hofstaeder's driveway. They had to kick Porky off the team for that, which was fine with him. Sports was kid stuff compared to the Real Thing, which was World War II. The team he wanted to join was the U.S. Marine Corps, and he was counting the days till his seventeenth birthday.

3

When the third and final bell rang I was in the back of the room with some of the guys, dramatizing my adventures at Mass that morning. Sister Raphael had to smack her ruler several times on her desk to stop the merriment and make us take our seats. Mine was the first one on the right-hand row, Kites had the last one in the same row, Roger and Elbows were at the other corners of the room. This was no accident; Sister had us separated as widely as possible to cut down on the horseplay. As an additional dampener she had us each hemmed in by serious, homely girls who wouldn't have dreamed of laughing in class even if they had known what was funny.

There were about thirty of us, half boys and half girls, divided into six rows of five. The desks had hinged wooden tops and fancy wrought-iron sides and were screwed to parallel strips of wood that ran to the back of the room. In high school, as a kind of status symbol, the desks were separate and were screwed directly to the floor. Another nice thing about high school was that you got to go to a different room and a different nun for each subject. In grade school we had to stay in the same seat all day listening to the same nun for the entire year. The only relief we got was an occasional guest appearance by Father Grundy for religion.

In such conditions the days could be stupefyingly dull, and anything that broke the monotony was devoutly to be wished. We were prisoners of war. Mischievousness was a means of preserving sanity.

I often wished that Sister Mary Jean was our teacher. She was pretty and friendly and not tense like so many of the others. The kids were always at their best when she was around because she somehow seemed to be on our side. She sometimes winked at me as if to let me know that she understood fully what it was like to be thirteen and trapped in a room with Sister Raphael. That may not have been her meaning at all, but there was no doubt about one thing: She was the best nun in the bunch by far. They had her stuck in kindergarten, where she couldn't be nice to anybody who counted.

Sister Raphael was the opposite of friendly, with a face that was chiseled out of cold flint. To her each day was a grim fight, to the death if necessary, to impose absolute discipline on her enemies. Although she was very small, she sat on two geography books and so presented a rather threatening aspect when glaring at us from her desk. But because the books made her taller sitting down than standing up, she seemed to grow shorter when she rose to her feet in anger.

We gave her plenty to get angry about. The objective of a good percentage of the class was to undermine the educational process to the fullest extent possible consistent with personal safety. The chief weapon was laughter—preferably someone else's. Most admired was the one who could convulse another without drawing attention to himself. Sometimes when Sister turned her back, several people at once would launch strenuous pantomime routines. Elbows, for example, would stand up as if to address the class and suddenly get shot in the stomach. He would sink back into his seat clutching his middle, his face twisted, and slowly expire, twitching. I had fair success pretending to throw up on the furniture and kids in my area.

If any of these efforts was rewarded by audible laughter, Sister Raphael would whirl around in outrage, which triggered an instantaneous restoration of innocent expressions. Anyone lacking the self-control to stop laughing caught the full

44

force of her fury, which usually took the form of a stinging slap on the face with her hand. Why laughter made her so mad I don't know.

When she was slapping me I imagined her as a Nazi camp commander. That way resisting her efforts to make me cry became a high patriotic act. I saw her habit as a black military uniform and her ruler as a riding crop. She was the notorious Bertha von Steiglutz, the Mad Bitch of Berchsdorff, who relished punishing Americans.

After a Hail Mary and a Pledge of Allegiance, the class buckled down to some intensive daydreaming while Sister reminded us for the thousandth time of the evils in the words "Xmas" and "hocus-pocus." It was par for a nun to have a well-developed sense of right and wrong, but Sister Raphael found sins in theological nooks other nuns didn't know existed. According to her, "Xmas" was an attempt to deny Christ a role in His own birthday and its prevalence was a grim reminder to all of us of the strength of the atheists and scoffers.

Her opposition to "hocus-pocus" was more technical, and its significance will be lost on those who have been denied a good Catholic education. It was her claim that the word was a corruption of the Latin spoken by the priest during the Consecration: *Hoc est enim corpus meum* [for this is my body]. With these words the unleavened bread changed to the Body and Blood of the Blessed Saviour in one of the most remarkable miracles God ever vouchsafed to Man. "Hocus-pocus" suggested that the Consecration

45

was a cheap magic trick, and therefore it was a term that had to be ruthlessly expunged from the language. She impressed upon us that anyone she caught using either of these expressions—plus others I have forgotten—would be subject to a revocation of recess privileges for the duration.

4

"Before we turn to today's civics lesson," Sister Raphael said, sliding down off her chair and walking to the front of her desk, "I want to tell you of an incident that happened to me as a girl that proves the tremendous power of prayer." I could no more think of her as a girl than I could imagine her sitting on a toilet. The whole class sensed that she was about to go through her "Lost in a Dakota Blizzard" story, and there was a restless stir in the room.

We were right. A few minutes later she and her brother, lost walking home from a Novena, had all but given up hope of rescue because of the snow, wind, cold, and darkness. I heard Elbows clear his throat, which was our signaling system. I couldn't look at him yet, though, because Sister was staring right at me. "That's when we remembered our rosaries," she said, "so we took them in our frostbitten fingers and began praying as we had never prayed before." She shifted her gaze to Patricia Alcorn, which gave me a chance to sneak a look at Elbows. He was sitting primly, his hands folded on his desk, a pleasant expression on his face, but with his eyes completely white! He had found a way to roll his pupils upward and lower his lids a little so that his eyes looked like two small snowballs! I had to laugh, and I paid the price.

For a moment I thought Sister hadn't heard me because she went right on with her story. As it turned out, she knew damned well who had laughed—she was merely trying to seem superior by remaining unruffled. She casually walked toward me and stood beside my desk. "Before long," she said, addressing the rest of the class, "a light appeared where only darkness and swirling snow had been before." She raised the ruler to shoulder level and gestured with her other hand for me to extend my palm. I did so slowly, bracing myself for the fire I would soon feel. "We struggled toward it," she said, still not looking at me, "although the wind seemed determined to hold us back. We fought forward, helping each other through the drifts, until we could see that the light was coming from a farmhouse. The Holy Spirit had guided us to safety."

I knew that she was almost ready to hit me. I looked up at her, studied the hard thin lines of her eyes and mouth. She was in her Nazi uniform now, about to bring her riding crop down on the defiant American prisoner.

("So. You are Shannon, eh? You are the one who won't tell us where your brother is hidden, eh? Do you enjoy pain, Shannon? Eh?")

("They don't call you the Mad Bitch for nothing, do they, Steiglutz? Well, I won't talk.")

47

("Ve have vays of making you talk, Shannon.")

("Well, they won't work with me, Steiglutz. Because I have something you can't take away from me, something you will never understand. I have faith in the Lord Jesus Christ and his Vicar on Earth, His Holiness the Pope.")

("Where is your brother, Shannon? Where is he?")

(I spat in her face.)

Sister Raphael turned to me and brought the ruler down with lightning speed. Crack! Pain shot up and down my arm, and my hand felt as if it had been seared with boiling grease. "Goddam you, Steiglutz," I muttered to myself.

"Soon we were wrapped in blankets," she went on in a calm voice, "sipping some good broth while the farmer cranked the phone to tell our parents that we were all right, that our faith in God and in our rosaries had saved us from the ravages of the storm." My eyes were tightly shut to hold back the tears. I bowed my head and put my throbbing hand between my thighs and held it there until the pain had passed.

That stupid blizzard story! No wonder the Jesuits thought the nuns were so silly. The Jesuits had been to college. They knew something. But the nuns, where had they ever been? No place. Father Brecht, who taught freshman religion at Loras College, always began his first class of the year by saying: "Forget everything any nun ever told you."

I looked at my hand and its red welt. She had

48

really whacked me! I had been hit before—a day seldom went by, in fact, that she didn't slap me at least once. Usually she simply hit people on the cheek with her hand. When she used the ruler she took it pretty easy. But this time she had put her whole back into it. I examined my palm and wondered if I could sue. The skin was broken slightly near the base of the thumb, which struck me as an important legal point. Maybe if I pressed the matter to a high enough court, justice would be done. VICIOUS NUN FOUND GUILTY—GETS CHAIR, the *Telegraph Herald* would trumpet in declaration-of-war type. The trouble was that before the case would come to trial the evidence on my hand would disappear due to the body's natural regenerative processes.

5

There was a knock on the door. It was Father Grundy. He wanted to see me. Me? Why me? Oh, my God! It was probably about this morning's Mass. That had happened so long ago I had almost forgotten about it. I walked apprehensively across the front of the room. My friends expected me to do a little smirking and mugging but I had all I could do to give them one wan smile.

When I neared the doorway the kindly old priest stepped into view with a maniacal look in his eyes that I didn't care for at all. Bringing his palm up from his heels he connected with a solid, stunning blow to the side of my face. It was by far the hardest I had ever been hit by a member of any of the religious orders, and my head reverberated from the concussion like a baseball that had just been homered. "That's for laughing in church," he said loudly enough for the whole class to hear. I moved my jaw back and forth to see if anything was broken. Now that he had hit me the expression on his face relaxed somewhat, but was still menacing. "You're staying after school tonight and you're going to write 'I will not laugh in church' one thousand times, do you understand?"

"F—Father," I gasped, "I wasn't laughing . . . I was coughing . . . I had something in my throat. . . "

"Stop it!" he shouted "Can't you see that lying makes it worse?" He had me by the shoulders now and was shaking me. He shouted some other things I can't remember, then let me go and began to calm down. His face, which had turned red during the action, returned to its familiar gray. He turned to Sister Raphael. "Thomas is to write 'I will not laugh in church and I will not lie about it afterwards' *five thousand* times, before he leaves the building tonight." When I heard that I could feel the fart-lighting slipping away from me forever.

"Yes, Father," Sister replied, nodding for me to go back to my seat, which I did gladly.

"Please forgive me for the interruption," Father said, looking saintly again.

"I welcomed it," Sister said. "Thomas is one of

several troublemakers in this class who have very nearly driven me to the end of my patience."

Before leaving, he addressed a few remarks to the class about how he would not tolerate any more disobedience, disrespect, and inattention from anybody, not just from me; how he would back up Sister Raphael to the limit in her efforts to enforce administrative rules, regulations, and policies; how a dirty, sniggering, disgraceful attitude had no place in an institution of Catholic learning where men and women who had pledged themselves to God were striving to inculcate into our moral fiber time-tested ethical precepts and who, if we would but let them, would equip us not only for this life but for the next as well, and how we should not take our blessings for granted while our fighting men were engaged in combat with an implacable foe so that we might be free to worship God the Father, who sent His only-begotten Son to die for our sins. Sister Raphael went on in the same vein after he left.

When the noon bell rang I sat for a long time staring at my inkwell before getting up to go home for lunch. Five thousand times! I would be stuck here writing till midnght . . . unless. . . . Already my mind had begun to probe for loopholes, for some way to fulfill the sentence but escape its consequences. . . .

"There's my big boy," my mother said as I slouched into the kitchen and collapsed into a chair. My father was somewhere behind an outspread *Des Moines Register*. "Are you all right? You look a little peaked."

"Huh? Oh. No, I'm all right, mom."

"Well, you'll feel better after lunch. The corn looks good today, and I made some pork chops and beef with gravy and pie crust."

Gravy and pie crust with two kinds of meat were one of the specialties of the house. It wasn't considered too heavy for the noon meal. We had three meals a day—the big meal, the huge meal and the tremendous meal. My father loved to eat, and he looked it. He loved to buy food, too, so he did most of the shopping. We threw out more food than most families ate. My mother couldn't get dad to stop buying so much food, especially meat. Apparently he couldn't get used to the idea that my brother was now being fed through the auspices of the federal government.

The steaming dishes on the table, my mother sat down. "Tommy served Mass in the big church this morning, Leonard," she said to my father, who rustled his paper in irritation. Then she said to me: "Well, tell us about it! You haven't said a thing."

"Oh, it went fine, mom. Yeah, great. It went fine."

After a few bites she said: "And how did school go?"

Jesus Christ, she was determined to have a conversation. "Oh, fine. Yeah. Nothing special. Same old thing."

Well, not the same old thing exactly. I fell on my ass, ripped the shit out of the Church Missal, and got my brains kicked out by sweet old Father Grundy. I would be running away from home soon if Hank Clancy didn't kill me before I committed suicide. Other than that there was little to converse about.

7

The ringing bell meant either that the place was on fire or that it was time for afternoon recess. It was recess. I nailed a few of my friends before they got out of the room and got them to agree to help me with my punitive writing assignment. Then I headed for the playground to persuade some of the sixth- and seventh-graders. In the corridor on the first floor I ran into Gretchen Schwartz, which cost me several precious minutes. She asked if she could borrow an eraser. As usual, she didn't have a stitch on.

"I just need it for a second," she said. "Do you mind?"

"No. Here." I handed her my pencil, glancing at her nipples and pubic hair. She hadn't spoken to me more than a dozen times in her life. Why had she chosen today? Was she, by some kind of telepathy, aware of the orgy the two of us had enjoyed the night before in my bedroom? Was she going to whisper that tonight she would be there again—not in my imagination but in the flesh?

"I have to turn in this theme in a few minutes," she said, applying the eraser vigorously, quivering from head to foot, "and there is this big old smudge right on the first page."

The night before, after tossing and turning in my bed trying to get to sleep, I gave up, lay on my back, and imagined that Gretchen was shinnying up the drainpipe on the side of the house. I turned my head and watched her climb through the window.

"Darling," she whispered, letting her dress drop to the floor, "I hope I didn't wake you. . . ."

I sprang out of bed. "Shh. My mother and father are in the next room and the dog is at the bottom of the stairs."

"I don't care, I don't care." She hung her panties on the crucifix and went to work on her brassiere, hands behind her back. It wouldn't come off. I tried to help, but her breasts were straining against their cups with such force that it was impossible to get enough slack to unhook the clasps. I finally had to use my Boy Scout knife while she pleaded with me to hurry. I carefully slipped the cold blade between her skin and the broad strap across her back. When I had sawed about half-way through, the rest ripped apart of its own accord and her breasts, free at last, sprang forward gloriously. They were bigger than I remembered them, and they jutted away from her body in heartwarming defiance of gravity. When she turned toward me her nipples swung in a wide arc, like gun muzzles scanning the horizon for bombers. "Oh, Tommy," she breathed, moving into me, flattening herself against my chest, touching the tip of her tongue to mine. . . .

"Thanks," Gretchen said, handing me my pencil. She tripped gaily down the hallway without looking back.

"Yeah, okay," I said.

. . . As my dick rose between her legs she clamped it with her thighs and slowly forced me backward and down onto the bed. She sat on my stomach and leaned forward so that when I opened my eyes I was faced with a fantastic panorama of swaying tits. Slowly moving her shoulders she dragged her nipples back and forth across my nose and mouth until I caught one gently between my lips. The other, with the full weight of its knocker behind it, settled into my right eye socket. Her tongue began to make love to my left ear and remaining eye while her left fingers tickled my nape and her right fondled my balls. I took these actions as a signal to clap my palms on her buttocks and thrust my pelvis toward the attic, effecting a complete penetration in a single, breathtaking stroke, at the same time wrapping my legs around her shoulders. Thus interlocked we hurtled through space like a revolving asteroid.

It may well be that this position is impossible

in view of what is now known about anatomy, physics, and common decency, but it nevertheless enabled me to achieve an orgasm of heroic proportions, an orgasm like a fireworks display. I was left limp and exhausted, and I drifted sweetly off to sleep.

8

I stared after her as she climbed the stairs and turned a corner, the coat-hook in my pants throbbing forlornly. Jesus, if only I could have banged somebody in those days! Just once! If only a girl could have seen her way clear to open her arms and legs to me and let me shoot off my gun without let or hindrance—what a relief it would have been! To have that relentless curiosity satisfied, to be free of that aching desire for a while—my grades would have improved, I know. I would have been able to relax a little and concentrate on my studies. I would have been more help to mom around the house, too.

Despite my own hunger, I recoiled at the thought of mom and dad having intercourse. It was so undignified, and they were so respectable. Of course, I knew they weren't tormented and lashed by lust as I was. They didn't have anything like my donk to contend with, which was so demanding and insistent that even God couldn't have gotten too angry with me if I had given in to it and criminally assaulted certain people. My organ was like a chunk of high-voltage cable from which the insulation had been rubbed. A dozen times a day it jumped up unbidden and strained to its full length, sizzling and snapping and trying to short out against anything female within range. When it was erect it seemed somehow unesthetic, out of scale with the rest of my body. I was afraid that a girl with any artistic sensitivity who saw it would either laugh or cry.

I was also afraid that it would one day be the death of me—a kind of death the details of which the *Telegraph Herald* would have to skip over. My vision was that I would get an erection that wouldn't stop growing. Bigger and bigger it would get, swelling and lengthening and sucking all the blood and juice out of my body until finally, a turgid obelisk of grotesque dimensions, it would explode, scattering debris on every girl I had ever seen.

What made life especially frustrating was that it was a sin to screw a girl unless you were married and had a job. In fact, it was a sin to even *kiss* a girl when you had a hard-on. Both Father Grundy and Brother Bartholomew had told us that—although they didn't say "hard-on." They used phrases like "a state of arousal." The point was that you could kiss a girl as long as you didn't enjoy it. According to them, a kiss, like a sincere handshake, was a perfectly acceptable sign of affection between two unmarried persons, but the instant it felt good you had to start saying Hail Marys or thinking about sports.

Another problem was that none of the girls of screwing age seemed to want to get screwed.

They were cagey, they never gave a guy a chance. And it was difficult to bring up the subject of screwing with girls who wore gold crosses around their necks and went to schools named Sacred Heart of Jesus, Immaculate Conception, and Blessed Virgin.

The girls were so different from the boys it was amazing. It was as if we were two separate species. The boys tried to glimpse forbidden lands down the necklines of blouses and under dresses, while the girls tried to keep such views obstructed. If you stood so that the sun was behind a girl wearing a summer dress, the outline of her body was sometimes visible in sharp detail, a treat she would never knowingly provide.

On a date, a boy watched for a chance to take a girl's hand, while a girl kept her hands out of convenient reach. Once the hand-holding stage was reached, a boy periodically offered an affectionate squeeze, which was never returned. A boy on a date thought constantly about the goodnight kiss and how to engineer it, while a girl, with exquisite timing, slipped inside her front door a second before he made his move. When a boy, through courage and perseverance, finally managed to kiss a girl, he tried to hang on forever, while a girl broke away as soon as she could do so without appearing rude. In a necking session a boy moved a hand closer and closer to one boob or the other, while a girl tried to keep her body twisted so that both were inaccessible.

With girls like these and a pud like mine, prospects for marital bliss were bleak. There was no way for the girls I knew to stop thinking of sex as a sin and start acting like the girls in my dreams, who threw off their clothes like confetti and seduced me with happy smiles on their faces. I knew what marriage would be like because I had once overheard Holy Mrs. Foley talking to my mother about it. "Isn't it terrible what we have to do to have babies?" she said. My mother nodded sadly.

So that's how it was going to be. On my honeymoon, when my bride would be required by law to let me make love to her, I would gather her into my arms and say, "At last . . . ," while she smiled gamely and thought, "Oh, ugh!" Later, in bed, my climax approaching like the Burlington Zephyr, I would gasp, "Oh my God! I love you!" while she thought, "Dirty, dirty, dirty . . . ," and began to pick out in her mind the style of twin beds we would have. What our Blessed Saviour had in mind when He instituted these differences I couldn't imagine.

CHAPTER FOUR

1

At five-thirty I was alone at my desk in the eighth-grade room racing the clock. It would be dark by eight-thirty, which gave me three hours to write "I will not laugh in church and I will not lie about it afterward" five thousand times. This was plainly impossible. The sentence can be written only about three times a minute, or one hundred and eighty times an hour. At that rate it would take me twenty-eight hours. But I had a plan.

Using a wire from the art supplies cabinet, I fashioned a series of loops to hold three pencils side by side—wrapping them with tape kept them from sliding up and down. With such a triple pencil I could turn out sentences at the rate of at least five hundred an hour.

On the playground, two floors below, were five of my friends equipped the same way. I had hoped for ten, but only five showed up, despite my bribes, threats, and promises. They were sitting on the ground writing on a long bench, using paper that I lowered to them in a basket tied to a string. Every once in a while I hauled up the work they had finished. I couldn't expect them to write at the same feverish speed I did, but if they would each turn out a total of six hundred sentences I would be in the clear.

My fifteen hundred combined with their three thousand made four thousand five hundred, which would be close enough because everybody was instructed to put a different number on each sheet. That made counting so difficult no nun would have time to do it. With novenas, meditations, litanies, and vespers they were kept hopping.

By seven o'clock I had done seven hundred and fifty and my crew fifteen hundred, but four of them had quit. Two said they had writer's cramp, one said he thought he heard his mother calling him, and the other, Patricia Alcorn's little brother Timmy, said he couldn't stay out any later because it was still only two weeks since his grandmother died. That left Bernice Vorwald, the Queen of Fat, who had always been stuck on me and would do anything I told her. It was mean of me to ask her to help me, because I had no intention of paying her back. If she thought I was going to take her out on a date in gratitude she had another think coming.

With half the time gone and my staff shattered, I was forced to boost output by slashing quality. I made two five-pencil holders with wire and tape and lowered one to Bernice, calling down to her to forget penmanship and aim only at speed. She nodded and bent over her work, her fat fingers flying across the paper. She may have been built like a tub of shit, but she was very dexterous. Every time I hauled up the basket I found that she had turned out every bit as much as I had. To keep her spirits up I waved at her occasionally so she would think she was on my mind.

At a quarter after eight, the sky alarmingly dark, and my arm shrieking in pain, I gave up. Sister's desk was strewn with papers. I don't know how many sentences were there—maybe four thousand. The last thousand or so were completely illegible but that couldn't be helped. If Sister Raphael figured out that there were too few, I would say that in my fatigue I must have miscounted. The widely varying handwriting I would blame on the different hand position I used to combat cramps.

The important thing was to get out of there before Sister came to check on my progress and deliver the inevitable lecture. Through past experience with impossible punishments I knew that at nine o'clock or so she would show up and bestow a magnanimous amnesty, expecting me to be grateful for it. I couldn't afford the time for a lecture just then. I knew that Porky and the gang were already gathering in the mower garage in the gulley below the seventeenth green.

I got out just in time. On the landing between the second and first floors I was trapped by nuns approaching from above and below. Into the trash can I climbed, as I had on another memorable occasion, assuming the foetal position amidst the debris of a hundred lunches. I held my breath until the nuns had passed and the coast was clear. One must have been Sister Raphael, because she went into the eighth-grade room. As I climbed carefully out of the can I heard her shuffling through the papers on her desk and clucking her disapproval. Well, I would face tomorrow's problems tomorrow.

I slithered down the first-floor corridor, my back against the wall, past the light coming from under the door of Sister Don Bosco's office. A moment later I was outside, darting in a crouch from one shadow to another until I was safely past the rectory and the church. I half expected the bell in the steeple to start signaling my escape. At the Hofstaeder's house I straightened up and fled like the wind down their driveway and over the back fence. I was free . . . free! Only a cornfield, Grandview Avenue, and an acre of alfalfa stood between me and the golf course.

2

The golf course—I can't begin to describe the importance of that golf course in my life. In the winter it was headquarters for skiing and tobogganing. We caddied there on summer days. On summer nights, ah, on summer nights it was a meeting place, a playground, and a refuge from the police. We could spike horns, steal fruit, break streetlights, and ignite piles of leaves with impunity when we melted into its vastness only to reappear a mile away, like resistance fighters from the sewers of Paris.

It was beautiful, the golf course was, and we knew its every wrinkle. The lush grass on the fairways and greens sprang from Iowa's black earth, which was conditioned in the winter by a blanket of snow and watered in the summer by weekly thunderstorms. The course was hilly, and the grass covered it like a rumpled blanket. It was ornamented by bunkers, sand traps, creeks, and clusters of elms, maples, and oaks. It was like a national park created with rich people's money to serve in perpetuity as a sanctuary for Porky Schornhorst's Raiders.

Because of the war, the cops were old and they were not track stars, so we were fairly safe. It was hard to get them out of their cars and almost impossible to get them to chase us onto the golf course, where they knew we could lead them into a dozen pitfalls.

A fairly routine thrill for us was the sight of our own shadows running ahead of us, shadows thrown by the beam from a squad car's spotlight. It was exceptional when the beam bounced from side to side, because that meant it was coming from the flashlight of a cop on foot. When we did succeed in getting the cops mad enough to run after us, a couple of kids always circled back to let the air out of the tires of their car or wire the engine with whistle bombs.

Under Porky's audacious leadership we sometimes used the country club's facilities for our amusement, like the swimming pool. It was surrounded by a six-foot chain-link fence topped by barbed wire, which hardly slowed us down. We crossed it in small groups with the help of a fifteen-foot ladder. When the ladder was leaning against the fence from the outside, projecting far above it, two or three of us would climb it until it tilted down like a teeter-totter. Once inside we pushed it back so the next group could cross.

We swam after eleven o'clock at night, when the clubhouse was dark and the neighbors were asleep. One night we sensed a trap, because although all the lights were out there were still several cars in the parking lot. We were sure an ambush was waiting for us when patrols Porky sent out returned with the news that two empty police cars were parked along the street a couple of blocks away. Porky whispered a few orders and we went into action.

Our three fastest runners, armed with boulders, crept stealthily toward the pool from the side bordering the woods. The rest of us, the smaller kids, took up positions well back in the trees, next to small stockpiles of fruit and vegetables filched from nearby gardens. At Porky's command the advance party heaved its rocks over the fence into the water and set up a chorus of happy shouts. Instantly the floodlights around the pool went on and a dozen cops and club members emerged from hiding places, confident that they had caught us at last in the act of splashing in their precious water and having a good time.

"All right, you kids," one cop shouted, blinking his eyes in the bright light, "get out of that pool and line up over here," a suggestion that was greeted by a rain of high-arching fresh produce from the woods. When the big guys got back from the fence we unleashed a tremendous barrage. Tomatoes, rutabagas, parsnips, and squash showered on the rich people and their Nazi officers from great heights. When they finally abandoned the field of battle in confusion and doused the lights for their own protection, we capped a perfect evening by chaining the bumpers of the two police cars together.

Other water sports for hot summer nights included "no nuts tag" using the green sprinklers. On a remote green like number five we replaced the sprinkler head with a nozzle and turned on the water with a wrench. We posted sentries and took off our clothes, leaving them in neat piles so they could be scooped up on the run if the need arose. The guy with the hose was "it" and the object for him was to avoid getting tagged, repelling his attackers with the powerful water jet. He could squirt you anywhere but in the nuts, because that might turn you into a girl for life. Porky was the champion. Once he got the hose it was practically impossible to get to him.

3

Porky was the gang leader not just because of his speed, toughness, and nerve, but because he was the best rock thrower. He was incredibly accurate, able to put out a streetlight at awesome distances. Sometimes his first pitch smashed the globe and his second the bulb. Seeing him hit a tiny light with a rock at a distance of fifty yards, plunging an entire neighborhood into darkness, was an experience not soon forgotten. Once he broke three streetlights with the same rock, recovering it each time from the broken glass on the street.

It sometimes took me half a dozen throws to break a streetlight, even if I was standing right under it. Porky treated such performances with the contempt they deserved, but he tolerated me because I obviously meant well and I tried hard.

A Porky Schornhorst feat that nobody in the gang could match was to stand on one side of Grandview Avenue and hit a telephone pole on the other side with a pickle, throwing the pickle in such a way that it passed through both open windows of a passing car. It took a great arm and perfect timing. One pickle Porky threw neatly removed the glasses of the lady driver. Because she turned out to be Roger Kenneally's aunt we found out that she was a nervous wreck for a week afterward. We thought that was funny at the time.

As caddies we had many ways of taking revenge on golfers we didn't like. Our favorite targets were Baldy Bemis, who owned the Bemis drugstores but never gave his caddy a tip; Wild Man Wunderlich, so named because of his reckless follow-through, another stingy rich bastard; and old lady Lindeman, who chewed out her caddy whenever she flubbed a shot. Such people deserved special retaliatory measures. It was not enough simply to step on their balls, pressing them into the turf.

Mrs. Lindeman lived in a mansion overlooking the second green. We tormented her by dragging a rake through the dew on the green in the middle of the night, spelling out giant obscenities that she couldn't help seeing in the morning when her maid was serving her breakfast.

Wunderlich and Bemis played together and were often the first twosome out on Saturday morning. We were able to spoil their entire weekend by crapping in the cup on number one. Sometimes they tried to outfox us by starting play from one of the other four tees near the clubhouse, hoping that somebody else would deal with whatever might have been done on the first green during the night. We met that challenge by calling on Kites Callahan to drop a turd in the cups on all four starting holes. Kites had superb control of his bowels.

For some reason, nobody in the gang was ever caught or found out. We seemed to lead charmed lives, like the commandos and paratroopers whose exploits we read about in the papers and were trying in our modest way to emulate. An example of the luck we had was the time eight of us piled into Mule Kahlbach's '36 Ford and drove over to West Third Street to steal cherries and grapes from the Borgward's back yard. Somebody called the police, because not fifteen minutes had gone by when a cop car came over the top of the hill. We jumped into the Ford and Mule released the brake before all the doors were closed. The open rear door on the curb side hit a telephone pole and snapped off, landing in the street. As the police swooped down on us from behind, their car ran over the door and got two flat tires, allowing us to make a clean getaway.

Mule was, in many ways, a fiend, and one feature of his car reflected it. He had wires splayed out under the upholstery of each seat so that he could give any passenger a shock by pressing a button on the dashboard. He had the chassis wired, too, to take care of guys leaning on the car from the outside. There is a dog in Dubuque, Iowa, that deeply regrets having pissed on one of Mule Kahlbach's hubcaps.

4

It was crowded inside the garage when I arrived and the air was murky with cigarette smoke. There were at least twenty boys there from St. Procopius High School, including several who had told me earlier in the day that they couldn't help me because they had to stay home . . . the pricks. The back of the pickup truck was filled with kids, and several pairs of legs were hanging into the light from the darkness above the rafters. No light escaped to the outside because the windows were covered with blankets and boards. There was no sound. Apparently I had come in at a crucial moment.

I had to climb onto the hood of the Massey-Ferguson tractor to see what was going on. Porky was sitting on the floor, the center of attention. His pants and shorts were around his ankles and his knees were drawn up and spread. With one hand he was holding his organs out of the way and with the other he was keeping a lit match and a box of matches in readiness. His face was lined with concentration, and he was muttering certain words over and over. I had to strain my ears and eyes to be sure I didn't miss anything.

"Come on, baby, come on . . . any time now . . . we're all waiting, baby . . . come on. . . ."

He was talking to his bowels, trying to coax a fart out. Instinctively I began to strain with him, like everybody else.

Kites was there, one of the inner circle of viewers. He was leaning forward expectantly, sweat glistening on his forehead, like a scientist about to see a comet that came just once in a lifetime. Kites could fart on demand, but he didn't have the nerve to do it into a lit match.

What would it be like? I wondered for the hundredth time. Would there be a long tongue of yellow flame, or would it be short and pointed and blue, like a blowtorch? Would it whoosh or pop or make no noise at all?

To get a better view I got up on my knees, and as I raised my head I knocked over a coffee can full of nuts and bolts. The clatter it made as it spilled over the hood and fenders was terrific, and everybody shouted at me at once.

"Hey!" "Jesus Christ!" "Who let him in?" "Knock it off!" "Shut up!"

Porky looked at me with the two black ball bearings he had for eyes. "Get him out," he said quietly.

"Who," I said, "me?"

"You. Out." He jerked his head.

"Aw, Jesus, Porky, I'll be quiet. I ran almost all the way to get here . . . you promised. . . ."

Porky glanced at his lieutenants to see why they weren't carrying out his orders. That's when the door of the pickup opened and I saw Hank Clancy. "I'll get rid of him," he said, moving toward me.

That big bastard! Why didn't he leave me alone? He probably told Porky a bunch of crap about me. He had no business here anyway—he hardly ever hung around with us at night. "Lemme alone, you big bastard," I said.

He threw a couple of guys out of the way and lunged at me, but I jumped to the floor on the other side of the tractor. I ran outside, hoping he wouldn't want to chase me and miss the main event, but apparently the thought of getting me in his hands blinded his reason. He came through the door like a bull charging into an arena. I took off across the fairway, dodging and ducking like a scared rabbit.

But I wasn't scared. For once I knew the odds were overwhelmingly in my favor. He was faster than I was on a straight line, but I was much more agile. An observer watching us racing around on the grass might have thought I was in grave danger, but in fact I had a choice of ways to put Hank out of commission. I knew the exact position of every rock, ditch, and stump on the course, and he didn't.

As I darted this way and that, listening to his curses and threats, I decided to put him in the water next to number fifteen green. That particular pond had a mud bottom and was enriched by sewage from the clubhouse. I headed for the edge of the bank overlooking the water, keeping track of my location in the night by watching the lights in nearby houses, by feeling the small but familiar changes in the slope of the ground, and by noting the feel of the grass as I went from rough to fairway to green.

When I came onto the green I slowed up a little and let Hank quickly close the gap between us. It was easy to adjust my speed so that he was only inches away from grabbing me as we reached the edge of the bank. I suddenly put on the brakes, dropped to the ground, and threw my shoulder into his oncoming shins. It was a tactic I had often rehearsed in my mind in case a cop ever got mad enough to chase me on foot.

It worked like a charm. Hank tripped over me and soared into the cool night air as if he had been launched from a catapult. Arms and legs thrashing wildly, he turned a complete somersault before hitting the water a good fifteen feet from shore.

When the gratifying sound of the splash came I

was already on my feet racing back to the garage. I was shaken from the collision but still in working order and still with a hope of seeing a fart lit.

5

But I was too late. I heard a blood-chilling scream, a scream I could somehow tell was Porky's, a scream that split the silence and sent people running to their windows for blocks around. The double doors of the garage burst open, the start of a desperate exodus. Within seconds, teenage boys were running in all directions in an effort to get away before men from the clubhouse came to investigate. The scream, several shouts that followed, and the light from the open doors would attract adults like flies.

I caught Kites by the arm as he tried to run past me. "What happened?"

"The matches went off between his legs—he burnt himself—lemme go. . . ." He tore free and ran toward a stand of trees and undergrowth.

"The fart . . . ," I whispered as loudly as I could, hands cupped beside my mouth, "did he light the fart?"

No answer. In a moment he was crashing through the brush with several others.

I looked inside the garage. Porky was duck-walking around in small circles, crying "Ow! Ow! Ow! Ow!" Only two of his trusted lieutenants were still there.

"Come on," one of them begged Porky.

"We've got to get out of here. This place will be swarming with cops in a minute. . . ."

"Ow!" Porky said. "I can't stand up! Ow! I can't walk! Oh, Jesus! Fuck! Ow!"

"We'll have to carry him. . . ."

They picked him up, one on each side, and staggered out the door with him. Porky stayed in a squatting position, unable to straighten his legs. He was breathing sharply through clenched teeth, and tears were leaking from his tightly closed eyes. I kept out of their way.

"Where should we take him?"

"To a doctor. He needs a doctor . . ."

"No!" Porky shouted. "How the fuck am I going to explain a scorched asshole to a doctor? Just get me away from here. . . . Ow!"

Too confused to think clearly, they carried him a few steps to the right, then a few steps to the left.

"To the woods by number eight," I volunteered. It was the shortest escape route and it would take us away from the water hazard, where Hank was probably slogging toward shore, dripping like something out of a monster movie. "We can get to Fremont Avenue through the hole in the fence by the fire house. Then we'll be only half a block from Doc McCready's house. He'll fix you up, Porky. He'll keep his mouth shut, too."

"Good idea," everybody agreed.

Doc McCready was a dentist who had been sued a year earlier by a woman who had come out of gas in his chair to find her blouse

75

buttoned-up wrong. Since then several of us had window-peeped and seen him feeling his baby-sitter. He wouldn't dare blow the whistle on anybody.

I started to lead the way but Porky told me to get lost, that it would be easier with three guys than four. He was right. One of the gang's first rules was to scatter when things went wrong.

"Okay, Porky. See you tomorrow." He didn't answer, but he knew who was with him at the end and who had thought of Doc McCready.

A few minutes later I was climbing the barbed-wire fence to the alfalfa field. Car doors were slamming behind the clubhouse, and I could see points of light bobbing from toward the garage—no doubt cops with flashlights. From far away in the other direction I heard a faint but anguished voice:

"What the fuck am I going to tell my old man?"

"Hot coffee. . . ."

"Yeah, you sat on a cup of boiling hot coffee. . . ."

"Aw, fuck! Ow!"

CHAPTER FIVE

1

February 22, 1944

Dear Mom and Dad and Tommy:

This is the first chance I've had to write in a long time. The action has been hot and heavy but we have them on the run. If the papers have been telling what my outfit has been doing, you might have guessed that I was in the Anzio landing. Don't worry, but I got a little nick in the foot. I am now in a hospital. Don't worry about it, because it isn't anything. It is very pretty here, especially the town of ——————. Did they cut that out? The chaplain says that all I can tell you is that I am in the general vicinity of ——————.

It is good to get a rest after a solid year. I sure have seen some things. I may get a chance to come home, but it is nothing to worry about.

Please send me some more fudge with

walnuts in it. The last batch was hard as rock when it got to me but I soaked it in hot water in my helmet and it helped a lot.

Yesterday from my window I saw ———————— ———————— go by in a jeep.

I hope Tommy is studying hard in school and not getting into any trouble.

Don't worry about me because I am O.K.

Your son,
Paul

My mother read this letter twenty times, and every time she burst into tears and said a rosary. My father read it only once, shaking his head and saying gravely, "I hope to God he's all right."

I don't know why this letter upset them so. I thought it was a wonderful letter, and I had a hard time hiding my excitement. He might be coming home! He would be a wounded hero with a Purple Heart! I could see him holding Porky Schornhorst's Raiders enthralled with stories of his combat exploits and donning his old basketball uniform to lead the alumni to a victory over the varsity. I could hardly wait to show him how much my hook shot had improved and to walk around town with him while everybody gawked at the ribbons on his chest.

A nick in the foot? That was nothing. He'd get over that. He broke an ankle once in a game against Oelwein and played a whole quarter on it before he said anything. He was tough as nails that way, but you wouldn't know it to look at him. He looked like a cream puff, with chubby cheeks and the beginnings of a pot belly. He always had a cheerful expression on his face even when fighting for a rebound. When he made a shot he chuckled, and when he was called for a foul he chuckled. He was the happiest guy I ever saw. I would be happy, too, if I was as good as he was underneath the basket; he could fake anybody out, I don't care who it was.

I could imagine him charging a machine-gun nest with a grenade, faking with his head and shoulders so the Germans couldn't keep him in their sights. "Ach! Who is this American who dodges bullets?" they would ask in bewilderment just before being blown to bits. "Who am I?" my brother would chuckle as the pieces rained down. "Why, I'm just 'Happy' Shannon from Dubuque, Iowa. Tell Der Fuehrer I'm coming to get him."

I daydreamed that later, relaxing in his foxhole, Paul would open the *Stars and Stripes* and notice an arresting headline:

EL TORO WIN STREAK STOPPED

San Diego (AP)—The El Toro Marine Base basketballers, despite the efforts of Joe Fulks and Mickey Marty, had their winning streak stopped at fifty-seven straight games last night by an unheralded Iowa high school quintet. The St. Procopius Apostles administered an 88-56 shellacking to the highly touted corpsmen. The Apostles were spearheaded by the incredible shooting of eighth-grader Tommy Shannon, who hit 100 percent of his field goal attempts en route to scoring honors of 44 points. . . .

"Well I'll be damned," Paul murmured.

"Shannon!" It was Captain Able Baker, whispering from a prone position.

"Yes, Captain?"

"There's a sniper on top of that cliff picking off our whole unit one by one. What should we do?"

"Get him, of course."

"Shannon! Come back here! Not you. . . . You'll never make it . . . not with your nicked foot. . . ."

"Take it easy, Captain, and read about my kid brother. I'll be back in no time."

A hundred pairs of American eyes watched him begin the torturous climb, and a hundred pairs of lips formed silent prayers. Hand over hand he made the agonizing ascent until finally his head rose slowly above the highest rock. The beefy German sniper was waiting, and pressed the muzzle of his Luger against Paul Shannon's forehead. . . . A rifle barked, the pistol dropped from fingers suddenly stiff, and the German slumped forward, dead.

Paul looked toward the sound of the shot and saw a grinning youth, smoke curling from an M-1 almost as big as he was. "You should be more careful, Paul," the lad said.

"Tommy! What are you doing here?"

Paul had written that he hoped I wasn't getting into any trouble. He didn't have much to worry about in the winter. In the winter it was almost impossible to get get into trouble in Dubuque, Iowa. It was hard to run through the snow, and if you tried you left a fine trail for the cops to follow. It was too cold to hang around outside very often, anyway. Another thing was that on weekdays Father Amos ran us so hard in basketball practice we were too tired to think about raising hell. On weekends leftover energy was spent dragging sleds and skis up the hills of the golf course. Hank was a constant threat, but Porky had warned him to keep his hands off me. Porky had not forgotten that I was the one who had found him a medic the night he got wounded.

When spring came—then there might be trouble. Schornhorst's Raiders would strike again. Risks would be taken, and somebody might fall into enemy hands. That would be too bad, but you didn't win wars by playing it safe.

The school day in winter often got off to a slow start because more time was necessary for taking off the extra clothes we had to wear. By the time the walls of the corridor were lined with galoshes and by the time the hooks in the cloakroom were loaded with leggings, snow pants, coats, mittens, sweaters, scarves, earmuffs, and caps, a good portion of the morning was gone.

We never missed a chance to steal minutes from our daily sentences in the prison camp of the Mad Bitch of Berchsdorff.

By the end of the day the halls were swampy messes from snow melting off the galoshes, and teams of high school boys had to make sweeps with wide mops so the water wouldn't get splashed on the walls when we marched out. We didn't just leave at the end of the day—we had to march out in a double file to the music of a Victrola while a nun marked time with a baton. We went through the front doors in strict discipline, even though we sometimes were going into the teeth of gales that broke our ranks as soon as we got outside. Heavily bundled up, we looked like so many balls of yarn.

A good thing about wearing a lot of clothes was that nobody could tell when you had a hardon. Of course, the girls were all covered up, too, so we didn't get as many. The most memorable one I got that winter was on a bitterly cold, clear Sunday afternoon on the golf course. I was there with my sled, along with a hundred other kids. The snow was perfect for fast coasting—the surface had thawed a little the day before and then frozen during the night into a shiny, icy crust. I had just arrived at the top of the hill next to number three green when a load of big kids on a toboggan came by, pushing themselves with their hands toward the brink. I put my hands against the shoulders of the girl on the end and helped push them into the start of their run.

The girl turned her hooded head and said,

"Thanks." It was Helene Hanson. There was a foot left on the end of the board, so without thinking I jumped on behind her, put one leg on each side of her and my arms around her waist. If I had considered it for even a second I would have chickened out.

"Hang on tight, Tommy," she said as the toboggan angled downward and began to gain speed, "these guys really go."

I could hardly believe it! I had my arms and legs wrapped around the girl with the most fantastic tits in town! If only we didn't have so goddam many clothes on. "Hang on tight, Tommy," she had said. I knew I would have her whispering that to me in my mind under my bed covers that night. Faster and faster we went, and harder and harder I got. Did I dare raise my mittens a little? Raise them so they were just barely touching the underside of her hypnotic overhang? Would she know what I was doing? If she did, would she care? It meant so much to me and so little to her, how could she care? Before I could find the nerve we were on the steepest part of the hill and moving at tremendous speed. The force of the wind took my breath away, snow spray lashed my cheeks, the sight of trees whizzing by in a blur against the whiteness of the landscape made me dizzy, and for a moment I was clinging to Helene for reasons of safety as well as lust. I pressed my cheek against the back of her collar and closed my eyes. We went over a small rise, and the toboggan left the ground completely. Despite the rush of the cold wind and the screams of those in front of me, I had a vision of Helene and me sailing through space alone, my flaming crotch glued to her rear end, my lengthening organ creeping up her spine. We landed with a wrenching change of direction, rocketed across a bumpy level area at the bottom of the hill, and began shooting up the hill on the other side. As we lost speed we veered sharply to the right and everyone was spilled onto the snow.

I opened my eyes and found myself lying behind Helene, still attached to her back. My left arm was under hers and my left mitten had come to rest, more or less of its own accord, on the general area of her chest. I couldn't be sure, but I think my hand was right on the storied wonderland of her tits! We had so many clothes on I couldn't orient myself exactly but as far as I could tell I was right on the money! If it hadn't been for my mitten and her coat, sweaters, shirt, slip, and bra it would have been the jackpot of a lifetime. I couldn't leave my hand where it was for more than a split second without arousing suspicion so I took it off, partly by lifting and partly by *sliding*.

"Wow, that was a great ride," I said for misdirection.

She was laughing as she got to her feet, apparently not having noticed anything untoward. Godammit, there may not have been anything untoward to notice. What I thought was a boob might have been nothing but a fold in her Mackinaw, but whatever it was it felt great through my mitten, and the creature in my crotch was straining

84

mightily to burst its bonds and spring into the sunlight.

"Come on, let's go," Helene said, running after the others, who were already started up the hill, pulling the toboggan after them. I had to let them go without me; I could hardly walk, much less run. I picked my way up the hill as best I could, taking short, stiff-legged steps, and when I got to the top they had already left on another ride. I picked up my sled and had a sudden impulse to make a flying belly flop to catch up. That would have been a disaster. In my condition I would have levered myself into the nearest drift.

I wandered off into a clump of bushes, trailing my sled behind me. My left hand went to my mouth and left a mitten between my teeth. By spreading my fingers in my pants pocket I enlarged a hole so that I could push through to the dark regions beyond. I pretended the icy fingers were Helene's. I pretended that she was pressing herself against me from behind, as I had pressed against her, her hand in my pocket, groping hungrily for what she couldn't do without a moment longer. Soon the inside of my shorts was under heavy mortar fire.

3

Getting erections at odd times of the day and night was quite a nuisance. Girls got the curse and that was no picnic, according to my cousin from Wahpeton, but they got it only once a month and it was more or less invisible. We had a theory that you could tell which girls were having "flag day" by the way they walked, slightly shorter steps being the giveaway, but we had no way of being sure. The whole subject of menstruation and sanitary napkins ("manhole covers") was out-of-bounds, and it was almost impossible to find out anything. Some of the high school guys who were going steady might have known something, but if they did they weren't talking. I knew what a Kotex looked like, at least, which put me a step ahead of most people. One summer when I worked as a stockboy at Hogan's grocery store I ripped open a box and gave its contents a close inspection, throwing them afterward behind the cases of pop bottles in the basement.

Girls knew when the curse was coming and so could plan for it, but when you had a dork you were never safe, as it was an involuntary muscle. Say you were standing in the hall talking to Sister Zita about how nice the Christmas crib looked and through the door of the cloakroom you caught a glimpse of Helene Hanson yawning and arching her back. Well, there you would be with a big wanger on, visible through your pants at fifty yards and proof that you had lost the thread of the discussion. What could you do? In a room you could put one foot on a chair, or sit down. Standing in a hallway your best bet was to lower your three-ring binder to your crotch in a natural manner.

Sometimes it was possible to "manage" your

boner so that it was less conspicuous. If you could get it over to one side people might think you had a sock full of nickels in your pocket. Or if you could twist it around so that it pointed straight up, flat against your body, it looked as if you merely had a rupture of the abdominal wall.

Some guys claimed they could stop the stiffening by controlling their thoughts at the first sign. If they were talking to Sister Zita and caught sight of Helene Hanson they would think about sports while blithely carrying on the conversation. Whenever I tried that my speech became unintelligible.

It was nothing special to get sexually excited a dozen times a day. It happened so often we had a joke about it:

"Did you see that car that just went by? It gave me a hard-on."

"Why?"

"Because everything gives me a hard-on."

I suppose if you were a millionaire or a movie director and could roll over and bang somebody every time you got a stiff on you wouldn't get stiffs on so often, but that option wasn't available to the eighth-graders at St. Procopius. The only legal relief we had was wet dreams, despite the problems they posed with mothers who did the laundry. In religion class we were told that in order to redeem the world God sent His only-begotten Son to Earth to live as a man and be sacrificed on the cross. Jesus was one-hundred-percent God, being the second person of the Holy Trinity, but was also one-hundred-percent man.

Arithmetic aside, did He have nocturnal emissions? Did His Blessed Mother know? We wondered about such things, but naturally you couldn't ask nuns or priests questions like that.

Then there was the illegal relief: masturbation, which we had to resort to in order to get enough sleep. If we hadn't whipped our puds once in a while we would have been walking around red-eyed with perpetual erections from one nocturnal emission to the next. The dilemma was painful: Lack of sleep was harmful to health, but masturbation was worse. Brother Bartholomew left no room for doubt. The boy who indulged in self-abuse, he told us, was sapping his strength, crushing the bloom of his youth, courting premature impotence, offending his Heavenly Father, and risking infections of the uretha. The beginning of the end, he warned, was the ejaculation of blood. That's why the sweet pleasure of pulling your pud was followed by waves of shame and guilt and fear. Mornings I searched my sheets for spots of red, and I studied my face in the bathroom mirror for signs of sagging skin.

Self-abuse was a deadly sin and was probably the worse thing eight-graders had to confess. I always confessed the number of times I had done it, but I didn't add any details. I didn't describe the hurdles I sent Gretchen over, and I never mentioned the life-size dummy of pillows I sometimes put together under the covers for purposes of assault.

In one respect the winter of 1943-44 was exactly like every other—our basketball team got slaughtered in the annual game with Dubuque Central, the public school. How I hated those smug, superior Prostestants and Jews! It was the biggest game of the year for us, but they treated it as a sort of scrimmage in which they could try out trick plays and untested grubs.

We thought we had a chance to win. We had edged tough Catholic quintets from Bankston, St. Donatus, and Apple River before trotting confidently into Public's huge gym, and in my opinion we had built up an irresistible momentum. I was wrong.

Central's All-State-Candidate center, Spider Ogelthorpe, played only the first quarter, yet made twelve points and grabbed every rebound at both ends of the court. Whenever an Apostle tried a shot, Spider blocked it so emphatically that on two occasions the ball bounced off his fist into the balcony. When they took him out, he sat in the bleachers laughing and talking with some Protestant girls in sweaters as if the game wasn't even worth watching.

Most of the time I sat in the middle of our cheering section shouting my lungs out whenever we made a basket, and withdrawing into a silent funk as Central poured in two or three in return. As I watched our players drop-kicking the ball out-of-bounds, shooting it over the backboard, and niftily passing it under the bleachers, it became clear that we were headed for a landslide defeat and I began thinking of forming a special commando task force that would come back under cover of darkness and break every window in the joint. Central wouldn't play so fucking well with a foot of snow on the floor.

What hurt was that I knew nobody would be surprised that they had run up a big score on us. On the surface they figured to have a much better team than we did because they had so many more kids to choose from. Dubuque Central had an enrollment of at least three hundred, while St. Procopius High School was lucky to count a third that many, including girls. St. Procopius was housed in a single, dark brick building, a big, dreary pile, but not so big that Porky couldn't throw a rock all the way over it. Central was a sprawling complex of gray granite towers and high walls that looked like West Point or the state penitentiary at Anamosa. Visiting athletes were scared half to death just at the sight of it. You had to give them credit for having a swell physical plant. Even their uniforms were impressive: silk in three colors. Ours were made of cotton so they could be put through the convent laundry, which gradually changed them from green to gray as the season progressed. We didn't even have enough to go around. Usually at least one Apostle had to wear his own undershirt and have a number improvised at the last minute out of adhesive tape, which by the end of the game would be half unstuck and flapping.

There was one thing we had, though, that they didn't. We had God. Our whole team went to Mass and communion the morning of the game. The Protestants and Jews didn't. Our players blessed themselves before shooting free throws and wore scapular medals blessed by the Bishop. The Protestants and Jews didn't.

Our team prayed during time-outs. I sat behind the Central bench for a while, and I know that they didn't. They put their hands together in a big knot just like we did, but they didn't pray. I could hear their coach. He said, "I want you to play heads-up ball and hit the open man. Keep your hands high on defense. Hit the boards hard. Set up your plays. Work. Fight. Move the ball. Okay, get out there and win."

In our huddle it was a different story; a different story entirely. Our coach and our players joined hands and spoke with one voice. "Hail Mary, full of grace, the Lord is with Thee," they said. "Blessed art Thou amongst women, and blessed is the fruit of thy womb, Jesus. Holy Mary, Mother of God, pray for us sinners, now and at the hour of our death, amen. *Let's go!*"

So not only did we have as much spirit and will to win as they did, we had a towering moral and spiritual advantage as well. And every year they beat the living shit out of us.

The only player on the Dubuque Central basketball team that I knew was Willie Richards, who lived in my neighborhood. He was a second-string guard and wasn't much of an offensive threat, but I suppose if he had decided to embrace the One True Church and transfer to St. Procopius he would have been our leading scorer. We could have used his height under the boards.

He was already a formidable scorer when it came to girls. They seemed to go for his blond curly hair, his muscles, and his confident manner. He and I often stood for hours under the streetlight in front of my house while he described his latest sexual conquest. I couldn't be sure he was telling the truth because I was never in the cars or on the sofas when the incidents were supposed to have taken place, but he included so many details he couldn't have been making it all up.

On Saturdays he sometimes took me with him to the YMCA. I never told anybody where I was going because I knew the "Y" was out-of-bounds for me as a threat to my faith. Even the Boys Club was considered dangerous because of the large numbers of non-Catholics that hung around there. I never fully enjoyed myself at the "Y" because I was always worried that somebody would make sarcastic remarks to me about the sacraments or the Pope. Nobody ever did, though. Either the employees and the kids who went there didn't realize I was a Roman Catholic or they were setting out to undermine my faith through an initial politeness.

What Willie did to me in the shower on my first visit wasn't very polite, but I know it wasn't YMCA policy; it was just something the members did informally on their own to newcomers. Whe he did was piss on my leg. We were in the shower with five or six other guys after a swim in the pool. I was facing one of the nozzles, soaping myself, minding my own business, trying not to look at anybody's organ. Willie was shouting in my ear over the roar of the water about the building's various recreational facilities. I thought he was standing awfully close to me, but I didn't think too much about it until I felt a weird warmth growing on my leg. When I looked down and saw what he was doing I jumped five feet in the air, almost knocking down a circumcised guy behind me.

Everybody in the room howled with laughter. They had pretended to take no notice of me, but actually they had been waiting impatiently for the initiation. I was mad as hell at first, but I soon saw the humor of it and laughed a little myself. Some of those non-Catholics were all right.

6

Winter came to a close on a melancholy note. The sun was warm, warmer than it had been in four or five months, and its light was blinding as it bounced off the melting snow still heaped on front yards. On the streets were shimmering, steaming sheets of moisture and the gutters were full of running water. Slogging through the slush in my galoshes on the way to school after lunch I met Elbows Hilken. He was wearing tennis shoes, so he stayed in the middle of the sidewalk, jumping over the occasional puddles.

"See that guy putting on shingles?" he asked, pointing at a man on the roof of a house hammering nails. "I'll betcha I can hit him from here." He scooped up a double handful of wet snow and began packing it into a ball.

"You wouldn't come close," I said, "and it would be stupid to try in the broad daylight. That guy looks mean."

"What's the matter, getting chicken in your old age?" With that he reared back like Bob Feller, and before I could grab his arm he had launched the snowball with frightening accuracy. The instant I saw how close it was going to be I started to run.

The snowball hit the roof a few feet to the left of the man's head and exploded all over him like a water bomb. He whirled around in a rage and, confirming my worst fears, scooted down the roof toward the ladder. He slid down it as if it were a firehouse pole and before I had a good start he was halfway to me. Elbows in his tennis shoes had a long lead but thanks to my galoshes, which my mother had insisted that I wear, I couldn't get up any speed at all. The snowdrifts and slush made darting and dodging impossible. I was, in

94

short, fucked. I churned along as best I could, hoping the buckles on my galoshes wouldn't accidentally become hooked to each other, the roofer gaining on me almost as if I were standing still.

I glanced over my shoulder and what I saw almost made me die of heart failure—the guy still had his hammer, and he had it raised! His face was a cloud of anger. He was coming so fast that he would be on me in a matter of seconds.

Fear engulfed me then, fear that started on the back of my neck and grew over my body like a wave of cold water. At that moment, without warning, I committed an indiscretion in my pants. I knew it sometimes happened to soldiers in combat, but I never thought it would happen to me. I didn't believe it *had* happened at first, but my nostrils soon offered unmistakable confirmation. My will to risist vanished instantly. I stopped running and stood rooted to the sidewalk, feet wide apart, fingers spread, a blasted expression on my face—a man in shell shock. I waited for the roofer's hands to land on my shoulders. Jesus Christ, if he dragged me to the police station like this the cops would have to mug me and book me with clothespins on their noses.

This wasn't the melancholy note I mentioned. That came next. The man I thought was chasing me ran past as if I didn't exist. He was after Elbows, not me. He must have seen Elbows throw the snowball—maybe he even saw me trying to grab his arm. At any rate, he paid me not the slightest attention. He was devoting all his strength to catching up with Elbows, who was about a half block ahead of him. I watched the two of them until they disappeared into infinity. Not only had I shit my pants, I had shit my pants for nothing.

School was out of the question, so I wobbled bow-leggedly home and told my mother it must have been something I ate. It was times like this that I appreciated my mother. She didn't make any of the cheap wisecracks I would have gotten from my so-called friends and perhaps even from my father. She was full of sympathy, and I appreciated it very much. She made me take off my clothes in the basement and after throwing my shorts in an ashcan washed both me and my pants off with a hose. Then she put me to bed, where I pretended to be sick for two days.

CHAPTER SIX

1

Springtime in Dubuque, warm breezes, budding greenery, and dogs following kids to school. Porky Schornhorst's Raiders were rolling again, my brother Paul was still enjoying life at an undisclosed Italian spa, dad seemed to have eased off the booze, and the Allies were advancing on every front. Eighth grade would soon be a thing of the past; the world seemed right.

The good news from the war fronts was greeted with mixed emotions by me and my classmates. We were beginning to worry that the war would be over before we were old enough to see action—a worry that drove us to ever more daring and desperate exploits at night.

And in the daytime as well. With summer approaching it was torture to be immobilized in Sister Raphael's classroom. I spent my idle moments trying to think of ways to get even with Elbows, who was still one up on me from the day he had turned his eyes white.

While Wanda Farney was reciting the procedure by which the veto power was exercised by the Executive Branch, I took a piece of paper and wrote across it: "Ellen Ettelsly is a rotten fuck." This was a disgusting thing for me to do. Ellen Ettelsly was the purest thing in the whole school. My mother wanted me to marry her someday, not just because she was smart and wholesome but because her father had a fine position in the County Recorder's office. She was always helping people with their homework and giving Spiritual Bouquets to her grandmother and stuff like that. It was repulsive enough to suggest that she fucked at all without adding gratuitously that she was rotten at it. My idea was to throw the message across the room to Elbows. He would laugh when he read it and get in trouble with the Mad Bitch of Berchsdorff or I was a poor judge of character.

My friends and I were fascinated by the taboo words for the organs and acts of sex. We used them all the time and even shouted them. Shouting them was risky—we did that from the top of the quarry south of Julien Dubuque's grave, overlooking the Mississippi. With nobody within earshot we could safely scream the most sickening, depraved, and blasphemous words and phrases in the English language, at the same time gesturing obscenely at trains and barges passing below. Shouting things we normally had to whisper had an exhilarating effect on us and we always ended up laughing giddily and feeling oddly purged.

We had learned from experience when behaving this way to keep plenty of distance between us and objects like trains and boats because we never knew when we would be recognized. Once when we were hiking outside of town Kites Callahan gave the finger to a freight train. To our amazement it slowly ground to a stop, couplings clanking and brakes squealing. The engineer climbed down from the cab and walked toward us. Just as we were about to turn and run we saw that it was Mr. Callahan, Kites's father! He had seen his son but, fortunately, had taken the finger to be a friendly wave.

"What are you doing out here at this time of day?" he asked. "Don't you know that supper's at six? Now get a move on." He took Kites by the shoulders and gave him a gentle shove toward town.

"Aren't you young Shannon?" he said to me.

"Yes, sir."

"Your mother will be worrying about you, too."

He waited until he was sure we were leaving, then climbed back up the ladder to the cab of the engine. The train left amidst great bursts of steam and clouds of black smoke. After that we shouted our curses and jabbed our fingers from the top of the quarry.

I finished my note about Ellen Ettelsly's inadequacies and folded it into a small packet. At that moment the most shocking thing of my life happened—the paper was snatched out of my hand by Sister Raphael.

If I had seen her coming I would have done anything to keep it from her—I would even have swallowed it. But I had temporarily lost track of her whereabouts and before I realized it she was on me like a black cat and had picked my hands clean.

"Don't read that!" I blurted out. "You'll be sorry . . . you'll really be sorry. . . ."

"We'll see who will be sorry," she said. "We will read this at the proper time. Then we will see who will be sorry." I clenched my fists and rose half out of my seat in frustration. "I've had all I can take of your tomfoolery," she went on, "and I'm going to put a stop to it." She put the paper wad on the center of her desk and addressed the class. "It is geography hour, children," she said cheerfully. "Take out your books and open them to page sixty-seven. John Myers and Evelyn Keane, would you please step to the blackboard and list the five most important exports of Uruguay?"

2

I couldn't take my eyes off the note on her desk. I had to get it back. If she read it and spilled it to my family, I was ruined. For writing such a piece of filth they might lock me up for life in the Eldora Reformatory. I kicked myself for not putting down what I had first thought of: "Bishop MacSwain was a muff diver." I might have been able to explain that away. I could say that Bishop MacSwain loved the water and that muffs were some kind of fresh-water anemone or some damned thing—but no, I had to go and write "fuck." There was no way to get around that—it was just plain dirty.

I eyed the note and wondered if I could get it if I made a sudden leap. No dice. She was sticking too close to it. I thought again of running away. Maybe I could live in the abandoned lead mines around Galena, Illinois. I thought about suicide, too. The room was about thirty feet above the playground and I was close to a window. If I made a run for it I could hurl myself through the glass and splatter my body against the teeter-totters below.

I tried to imagine what Sister would do when she looked at the note, but I couldn't. A nun reading "fuck"? She would probably make me apologize to everybody under the sun—to Ellen, to her mother and father, to my mother and father, to God knows who all. If I had to do that I would never be able to look any of them in the eye again. I didn't see how I could even acknowledge the existence of the word "fuck" to a grownup. What was I supposed to do, walk up to Mr. Ettelsly and say, "Sir, I'm sorry I wrote that your daughter is a rotten fuck. Actually, she is a terrific fuck." No, there was just no way. I would have to get that note back whatever the cost.

Several funny things happened in the next few minutes, but I didn't feel like laughing. Sister Raphael, announcing that it was time for art, opened the cabinet where the supplies were kept and half of them fell on the floor. It sounded like Fibber McGee's closet and I heard strangling noises in the room as people tried not to laugh. I didn't think it was funny at all, which shows the psychological state I was in at the time.

Then Elbows cleared his throat. I didn't want to look. I didn't need any more trouble. But I slowly turned my head toward him nevertheless, partly out of habit, partly out of respect for the bonds of loyalty that held us together despite our differences. He was looking at me with a grin. He must have had a fine thread looped over each ear leading to his hands beneath his desk, because he was making his ears flap up and down. It was one of the goddamdest sights you would ever want to see, but I was too emotionally spent to give him the slightest flicker of response.

Sister Raphael, however, responded with vigor. She was on him at once with her ruler aloft. "I saw that, Mr. Smart-aleck," she snapped. "Put out your hand."

He didn't. He stared at her defiantly, which he could afford to do because if he got kicked out of school he would simply start work in his father's gas station two years ahead of schedule. "Put out your hand," she repeated.

"No," Elbows said. He was big for his age and his eyes were almost at the same level as hers, even though he was sitting down and she was standing up. He looked much older than he was and even had a faint, silky moustache. Sister had one herself, as far as that goes.

Suddenly she pracitcally screamed at him to put out his hand. Her voice was much higher and shriller than usual—she was obviously losing her temper fast, so everybody sat up and took notice. Elbows, still staring at her, slowly brought his hand out from under the desk—with a baseball glove on it! When he extended that for her to hit, she seemed to explode and she did something I had never seen her do before—she let him have it right in the face with the ruler.

"Watch out who you're hittin'," he said, jumping to his feet. She swung at his face again but he blocked the blow with his forearm. "I said watch out who you're hittin'."

She made some kind of sound—a groan—as she turned away and walked unsteadily back to her desk. The ruler slipped out of her fingers and clattered to the floor. Her eyes were glistening and her lips were trembling. I think she was crying! Elbows was the one who got hit, yet *she* was crying. She sat down on her two geography books and tried to get control of herself. She looked vaguely toward the back of the room, breathing heavily, blinking the tears away, and pursing her lips over and over. I began to feel a little sorry for her. She didn't understand us and we did give her a pretty hard time, but Jesus Christ, there was a war on and we had to have some fun.

It took five or ten long minutes of silence before she quieted herself down and regained her composure. I sneaked a glance at Elbows. He was sullenly rubbing his cheek, looking as if he had decided against pursuing his education any further. Finally Sister spoke. Her voice was strangely small. It was impossible to imagine such a tiny sound coming from Bertha von Steiglutz.

"Harold Hilken," she said to Elbows, "you will stay after class and you will come with me to the rectory. Father Grundy will decide what will be done about your disgraceful behavior." She turned to me and held up my note. "I am going to give this to Sister Don Bosco for disposition as she sees fit." She stood and put the note, along with whatever hopes I had of recovering it, into a deep, secret pocket in her habit. Then she dismissed the class, even though there were still five minutes until the noon bell. It was the first time we ever got out early.

3

Lunch was a familiar scene. Dad behind a paper, me slumped over my plate worrying about worsening personal problems, dipping pieces of pie crust into gravy without enthusiasm, and mom chattering happily as if people weren't suffering and dying all over the world. Every once in a while dad rattled his paper to show that he would appreciate a little less noise.

"And how was school this morning?" my mother said at the end of a long spiel about something or other.

"Yeah," I said.

"Fine?"

"Yeah."

After a pause while she filled my glass with milk she said, "Was Ellen there today?" She tried to throw that out casually. She was always trying to remind me of Ellen in various obvious ways.

"Huh?"

"Have you heard a word I've been saying? I asked you if Ellen was in school this morning."

"Oh. Yeah, I guess so. I didn't really notice."

I didn't really notice, but I had filed a written affidavit to the effect that she was a rotten fuck.

4

My father and I stood looking down at my uncle, who was hip deep in the nauseating muck of the B Branch Sewer. Uncle Ed was the foreman of the B Branch Sewer project, one of the few city jobs my father had that year. City money had pretty much dried up, and my father and his crew were keeping busy mainly with cost-plus jobs for the railroads, widening and strengthening bridges so they could take heavier military loads. It was common to see long trains rumbling through town loaded with tanks and artillery and mysterious shapes shrouded in canvas. Troop trains came through, too, at all hours of the day and night, usually so covered with dust that you couldn't tell if they were empty or full.

The B Branch Sewer couldn't wait till the end of the war. It was an open channel that in hot weather not only stank to high heaven but served as a breeding ground for dangerous, disease-carrying insects and rodents, according to an expert from the University of Iowa. My father's job was to put a concrete lid on it from the packing plant through the city dump to the point where it debouched into the river just above the public beach. The Leonard E. Shannon Construction Co. (my dad) had won the job with a low bid of forty thousand dollars, edging out Bud Paul and Fred Schwinn, which was no surprise to me because I had heard my father tell them on the phone that if he could have the sewer job they could drive the piling down at the harbor.

After lunch my father had told me to get into the car, that he would give me a ride back to school after he "stopped by the job." When he told me to do something I did it—my buttocks still tingled from a spanking he had given me three years before. We rode to the job in silence. I had plenty to think about, none of which I could discuss with him. He had his work to occupy his mind, along with American Legion politics, and he knew there was nothing helpful I could say in those areas.

Dad showed me the B Branch Sewer job at least once a week, and I knew why. He wanted me to see what kind of work people had to do who didn't finish their schooling. Uncle Ed, for example, was highly regarded as a cement finisher and stonemason, but there he was, wading around in noxious effluvia because he couldn't read blueprints. If I would get serious about school I could go to college and become a civil engineer and sit in a nice office somewhere like Vern Schiltz or

Kenny Cullen, while if I went on treating school like a big joke and a big game, why then sure as hell I would wind up like Uncle Ed, up to my ass in God knows what.

Dad didn't tell me such things in words. His way was to let me see the facts with my own eyes and draw my own conclusions. It worked, too. The lesson he was trying to teach me was one I hated to learn, but after a visit to the B Branch Sewer I was usually quite sober for a couple of days, as well as faintly sick to my stomach.

I must have been the picture of discouragement—hands in pockets and head hanging—because my uncle and several of the other men made a point of saying hello to me. I don't know if they were really glad to see me or if they were just afraid I would be the boss some day. I tried to cheer up and pretend I had no problems and didn't notice the odor that was everywhere.

"Too bad you have to go to school this afternoon, Tommy," Uncle Ed said to me with his usual very serious expression. "I dropped my hammer somewhere in this stuff. You could dive in and help me find it." This brought a chuckle from some of the other men.

"I think I would rather do my regular jobs, Uncle Ed," I said.

My regular jobs when I worked for my dad were to keep the water bucket filled, tend the wood stove in the construction shack, pound nails out of boards and straighten them so they could be used again, and scrape mortar off used bricks.

While my father tried to attract the attention of

the city inspector away from what the men were doing, Uncle Ed explained to me that the first part of the job, putting in the timber supports for the roof slab forms, was the worst because the men had to stand in the sewage. The concrete work would be done from above, and wouldn't be bad work at all. He was the only person who ever told me what was going on, which was why he was my favorite uncle.

5

Uncle Ed had a lot of dignity. He carried himself with great aplomb despite his work clothes and battered hat. The other men were always cursing and hurting themselves, but not him; he went about his chores on a higher plane, with the quiet confidence of a great artist. He was at his very best digging ditches. If you walked along a trench in which my father's crew had been digging you could easily spot Uncle Ed's section because it would be neat, flat, dry, and clean, with the walls perfectly vertical and showing a regular pattern of scallop marks made by his shovel. He kept the edge of his shovel sharp so that it cut smoothly when he stepped on it with his boot. A slight levering of the handle and he broke out a neat packet of dirt that could be handled without spillage and could be lofted through the air as if it were wrapped in paper. The long pile of dirt he left at the side of the trench was so even it looked as if it had been laid down by a machine. Rocks were no problem to him because he knew exactly where to strike them with his chisel so they would break into handy fragments.

His skill showed up dramatically in a wet trench. With several inches of water at the bottom the other laborers would be slogging about in slime, covered with mud, while Uncle Ed would be unruffled and unsoiled, standing on a dry platform of dirt that he had left for the purpose. The men on each side of him often edged closer and closer to take advantage of the neat, convenient steps and layers he created for himself. Possibly he was the greatest construction worker in the world.

CHAPTER SEVEN

1

My father was driving me to school after our noon-hour visit to the B Branch Sewer. I sat quietly, working on my courage, for I had decided to tell him about some conclusions I had reached after a lot of serious thought. Finally I spoke.

"Dad, I'm going to start doing better in school. I don't want to work all my life with a pick and shovel. If you have to go to college to get a good job, then I want to go to college. I know I can do it. I may not be as smart as Ellen Ettelsly or Richard Carew, but they study all the time and have big sucks with the nuns. I just want you to know that I'm going to try harder. I really am."

It was a hard speech for me to make, and my voice was quavering a little at the end. I had never said anything so important or personal to him before and I wasn't sure how he would take it. It was embarrassing to be so sincere with your own father. I felt myself reddening. My words had sounded a lot sillier than I thought they would, and I wished I had kept my mouth shut.

111

Fortunately, he didn't hear me. He kept right on staring at the road ahead, lost in thought. He was out of the habit of listening to me and perhaps assumed that I had made another comment about high school basketball, a subject that didn't interest him greatly. It was just as well; I knew what he would have said. He would have said that I was finally showing a little sense and that since I had to go to school anyway I might as well get as much as I could out of it and that he wanted me to go to college even though he didn't know where he would get the money. I would say that maybe I could get my brother's old job of delivering milk and he would say that he wished I would get some new friends, as I would never amount to anything hanging around with that Callahan kid with the big ears and the rest of his bunch. All of these things were perfectly true and we both knew it, so I guess there wasn't much point in discussing them.

My father usually wasn't very good company until about four o'clock in the afternoon. By then the effects of a few too many highballs the night before had worn off, the day's work of being angry with his men was finished, and he could look forward to a couple of hours of relaxation with the *Telegraph Herald*, a fine big meal, and some games of euchre at the Legion, with a few too many highballs again. By the time we sat down for supper he was in great spirits, even jovial, and often kept us laughing continuously with stories about people the whole family knew or had heard of. Other contractors, the city council, the county supervisors, relatives, farmers, the clergy, and drunks were favorite subjects for anecdotes—anecdotes made memorable by his animated manner of telling them and his hoarse, all-embracing laughter. He was especially good at describing how respected local rich people had got their money. The Borgwards, for instance, who owned the sash and door factory. According to my father, they struck it rich in the early days of Dubuque County by obtaining an easement from the government to cross federal lands between Dubuque and Sherrill's Mound, twenty miles away, where they planned to open a limestone quarry. The written agreement made no mention of the width of the road, so old Felix Borgward, who lived on until 1907, made it one mile wide and sold all the timber.

One of Felix's grandsons was a problem child, my father enjoyed pointing out, unable to hold a steady job even at the family factory. The Borgwards had managed to keep him out of the army by putting a majority of the draft board on retainers as Planning Advisors for the company, after which the board ruled that Felix III's membership in the Knights of Columbus was an essential occupation.

2

Although my father entertained me at supper and occasionally urged me to do well at school so that I could go to college, he took no active part

113

in my education, aside from exposing me to various dead ends he wanted me to avoid. He mentioned sex to me only once and that was after a week of urging by my mother, who had become alarmed at evidence of nocturnal pollution in my sheets three nights running. I had turned twelve two weeks before.

"You've got to talk to Tommy, Leonard," I heard my mother say one night when they thought I was asleep. My father mumbled something in reply, hoping she would change the subject or forget it. "He's growing up," my mother insisted, as though she knew it sounded unbelievable. "I've seen him staring at girls in church. I've noticed . . . other things, too. You simply must talk to him. Some warnings can only come from the father. You know what I mean. You wouldn't want me to tell him, would you? He would think you were afraid to. Promise me you'll do it this week."

Seven days later he was waiting for me in the kitchen as I ran breathlessly into the house after basketball practice.

"Hi, dad. Home already?"

"Sit down, Tommy," he said, looking as though he were suffering from a vague pain. "I want to talk to you about something."

"Gee, dad, what?" I sat down gaily, pretending I didn't have the faintest notion of what was coming. "Boy, am I pooped," I said. "Father made us run around the gym twenty times. In the scrimmage with the big guys I made four points."

"Oh? Good." Still standing, he rested the heels

of his hands on the edge of the table and stared at the toaster.

"I took the ball away from Lester Vorhees once, too. Boy, was he mad. He practically knocked me down trying to get it back. But Father blew the whistle on him and gave me two free throws."

"Oh?"

"I made the first one and I should have made the second one, too. It looked good all the way."

Dad went to the window and regarded the shrubbery sadly while I rattled on. I didn't intend to give him an opening. If I could keep talking long enough something was bound to happen to interrupt us—maybe mom would come back from wherever she was, or the water heater would explode again, or the dog would die. But nothing happened except that I soon ran out of things to say. When I fell silent at last my father took a deep breath and looked me in the eye for the first time since I had come in.

"Fine. But there is something I have to tell you." He sat down across from me.

"Well, gee, what, dad?" I didn't know exactly what he was going to say, but I was terribly afraid he was going to bring up the matter of my sheets. I began to flush and I could feel my eyes getting ready to water if they had to.

"Maybe I should have told you this before."

"Told me what?"

"But sometimes too soon is as bad as too late. Your mother and I, that is, she . . . or rather, we, have noticed, well, there is something you've got to understand." He shifted around in his seat and began again. "Look, you are a good boy. I know you wouldn't want to do anything wrong. You're not dumb. The Shannons are not dumb. So I am only going to tell you this once. Then we won't talk about it any more because I know I can trust you and I know you are not dumb. And I know you want to do what's right."

I looked at him with eyes as round as I could make them. It was an excruciating moment for both of us.

"Tommy, listen. Don't monkey around with girls because you can get all kinds of terrible diseases."

As soon as he had said that he got to his feet and went down the stairs to the basement and began driving nails into a loose board my mother had been complaining about.

3

When I was in the eighth grade my parents were in their fifties and overweight and I couldn't for the life of me imagine them engaged in sexual congress. My cousin from Wahpeton several years before had tried to convey to me the basic outline of how babies were conceived, but I fought against the idea. I couldn't picture mom and dad doing such a thing. Taking off their clothes and lying down on top of each other? Ridiculous. They didn't even dance. What he was trying to tell me, in fact, was disgusting, and if he hadn't been bigger than I was I would have beat hell out of him for putting the thought in my head. Not that he ever mentioned my mom and dad; in his examples he was always careful to use two hypothetical people from Wahpeton.

As time went by and evidence favoring my cousin's theory continued to come in, I finally had to admit that he probably had something. I myself was proof that my parents had fooled around with each other in some manner at least once, and my having a brother tended to suggest that there had been another occasion. An only child might have been able to entertain the possibility of a virgin birth, but belief in two in a row was too much to ask even of the most devout.

I don't mean that my mother wasn't saintly enough to receive special attention from God, because she was—otherwise I would never have written that letter proposing her for canonization. Her figure was matronly rather than ascetic, but there was something ethereal about her face and its halo of gray hair. A person who worked as hard and as unselfishly as she did and said as many rosaries every day had to be getting help from somewhere. She had a way of pausing while doing the dishes and turning her face to the light streaming through the window, peering for a moment into the far distance—into infinity. I think it was then that secret strength flowed into her.

Watching her stoke the furnace on a gloomy, bone-chilling winter morning—as I often did while sitting at the top of the cellar steps—left no doubt that she was somehow beyond the natural

117

order. The furnace dominated the basement, its asbestos arms held high, as if ready to drop on an unsuspecting victim. When a fire was going, draft holes in the steel door glowed like dull, red eyes, making the whole contraption seem alive and malevolent.

It ate coal—coal that was brought to the house in a huge, filthy truck. Two men used a steel chute to send the black lumps through a basement window into our dilapidated wooden coal bin. The clang of the shovels and the roar and boom of the coal as it cascaded down the chute and crashed into the wooden walls sounded like an artillery barrage.

It was easy to think of our furnace as the embodiment of the Forces of Evil, while my mother, in her flowing nightgown, brandishing a lancelike poker and a shining shovel, was Joan of Arc. When the furnace door was open and the fire within was raging, lights played on her face and grotesque shadows danced behind her. It was as if she were engaged in a death duel with the devil in the bowels of Hell itself.

The Church demanded more of its saints than simple heroism; there had to be an element of the miraculous present as well. In my mother's case I could point to two things. One was that even though everything in the basement was covered with a layer of dust from ashes and coal, not a speck of it ever got on her. She could work there for half an hour and return to the kitchen spotlessly clean. My father and brother, on the other hand, looked like chimney sweeps after five minutes. A mysterious force shielded my mother.

The other thing was that she had an uncanny ability to guess the number of beans in a jar. At county fairs and church bazaars her estimate was almost always the best. Sometimes she hit it right on the very bean. "Oh, I'm sure I wouldn't know," she would say with a shrug, looking at the jar. "I wouldn't have any idea. Maybe sixteen hundred and seventy-eight." And she would be right! It was fantastic.

These were the points I planned to stress if the College of Cardinals balked at bestowing on my mother the high honor so plainly due her. Balk they might, because she had weaknesses. She lost her temper once in a while, mainly when my father drank too much and came home late, and that would certainly count against her. Another thing worried me. In *The Lives of the Saints* nobody had any kids. Nobody even seemed to be married. But if a family threatened to hurt her chances, then I was prepared to deny that she had one. Such a lie would no doubt consign my soul to eternal damnation, but that was probably going to happen anyway for other, unrelated reasons.

CHAPTER EIGHT

1

Dad dropped me off in front of school about five minutes before the start of afternoon classes. I waved good-bye and walked disconsolately toward the door. I had a lousy day ahead of me. The thought of my intercepted note being opened for a dramatic reading by Sister Don Bosco took the fun out of living. What I didn't realize was that an attempt was about to be made to take my life out of living as well.

Hank Clancy had spent his noon hour enlisting in the Navy, and was crouched in the bushes outside the front door waiting for me. He felt free to revenge himself on me now because in the Navy he would be out of Porky's reach.

At the front steps Kites Callahan asked me a question that probably saved my life.

"Hey, have you got that book today?"

Jarred out of my reverie, I looked at him over my shoulder, and that was my salvation. Out of the corner of my eye I saw Hank, teeth bared and hands like claws, sailing through the air toward me. His time had come at last.

The book Kites wanted was *Manual of Nursing* by Braddock and Sylvestri. I had found it while snooping through the closet and drawers in my parents' bedroom. It was at the bottom of the cedar chest, under the mothballed quilts, and it contained some of the most lurid illustrations in the world. One I will never forget was a series of cutaway drawings of the uterus showing Catholics in various stages of development, with the *vaginal canal* labeled as plain as day. Because of that book I was, at age thirteen, a kind of half-baked expert on the anatomy of the human crotch and the ills it was heir to. There were serious gaps in my general medical knowledge, because I confined my reading to erogenous zones, unable to sustain interest in other chapters, though I had no reason to question their scholarship. Besides, the book itself was incomplete. It went into great detail on how the foetus escaped from the womb, for example, but it didn't have a single word on how it got in there in the first place. The result was that while I was a blank on eyes, ears, noses, and throats I knew as much about delivering babies as your average, run-of-the-mill doctor.

As far as gonorrhea, syphilis, and other veneral infections were concerned, Braddock and Sylvestri provided me with a vast stock of information on diagnosis and treatment, but they left unanswered the one question that was sure to be on the mind of every reader. Were the pains, inconveniences, and dangers inherent in these diseases worth the pleasures to be derived from contracting them, or were they not? That's what I wanted to know.

"No, I didn't BRING IT," I said to Kites, shouting the last two words because of the sudden effort I had to make to dodge Hank. One of his claws gripped my arm briefly, but I was able to twist free.

"Oof!" he said, as he jackknifed over a waist-high steel railing.

"Holy Christ!" I said. I raced up the stairs and knocked the books out of the hands of Richard Carew, who was opening the door in front of me.

"Goddammit," said Richard Carew.

"You little bastard," said Hank, recovering quickly and coming after me.

"Bring it tomorrow, will you?" Kites shouted. "I want to show Herby the pictures of that guy with all the scabs."

2

I reached the Band Room on the third floor with just enough time to scoot into the secret room under the screens before Hank burst through the door. He dove to the window, sending rickety music stands clattering in all directions. I wasn't on the rain gutter or the fire escape. He threw aside the curtain to the nuns' quarters and looked at an empty corridor. Then he slowly turned, satisfaction growing on his face.

"All right," he said, "you're in here some-where. . . ."

He didn't scare me. He wouldn't find me in a million years. I was completely safe in my co-coon.

He stared at the screens. He moved several to one side. "You must be in there," he said, as if answering my thoughts. "It's the only place you could be."

He began peeling screens away, layer after layer, throwing them aside noisily. I could hear footsteps coming up the stairs, but they would be too late. When he got to the last screen, the one that would reveal me quivering like a chrys-alis in the sun, I did the only thing I could—I picked it up myself and threw it at him.

"Hah!" he said, parrying it easily and jumping to the door to cut me off.

But I wasn't headed for the door. I went for the window and was through it like a flash. To my horror the fire escape was blocked by a nun in an apron on the landing below who was shak-ing a dust mop. She looked up at me in surprise. I sidestepped quickly in the opposite direction along the rain gutter until I was outside the reach of Hank's hairy, groping arms. I flattened my back against the roof, which rose almost verti-cally between the dormer windows, much too steep for climbing. In the sky several enormous clouds were drifting slowly toward Wisconsin. I gazed at them, trying not to think of the ground forty feet below.

"Come in off of there, you dumb fuck," Hank said.

I swallowed and wet my lips, not looking at him. He started to come after me, climbing through the window. When he put part of his weight on the ledge it sagged and groaned ominously. I sank my fingernails into the shingles and felt the major muscles in my body freeze.

"Holy shit," Hank said, withdrawing his foot as if it had been burned.

The nun on the fire escape squeaked, dropped her mop, and fled into the building. On the playground three kids on swings were pointing at me.

The view was wonderful from where I was. I was higher than the roof of the convent, so I could see over it to the Mississippi several miles away. Sunlight was reflecting off the water and off the yellow limestone cliffs along the Illinois shore. In every direction there were green hills, green fields, and green stands of trees. In the summer the whole state of Iowa was a garden, with all kinds of growing things crowding out of the black earth. The city of Dubuque, though, aside from its tree-lined streets, wasn't much to look at. Too many drab brick warehouses and factories, too many rows of wood frame houses in need of paint. The only beautiful thing in town was Eagle Point Park, which was built by the Work Projects Administration during the depression.

According to my father, a world-famous traveler had once stopped in Dubuque on his way to someplace else. "Nowhere on this planet," the famous man said, "is there a city like Dubuque, where God has done so much and man so little."

"What's going on here?" It was the commanding voice of Sister Mary Don Bosco, the principal, from inside the room. "Henry Clancy! What's the meaning of this? Were you the one who thundered up the stairs like a stampede of cattle? Did you make this mess?"

"Yes, he did," said the voice of Clara Weems, one of the sucks and squealers. "I saw him."

"All right, Mr. Football Player, then you are going to clean it up. When you are through report to my office. I will not tolerate maniacs in this school."

Her head was out the window, looking at me. "My heavens!" she said. "What on earth. . . ." She glanced at the ground, then back at me. "Thomas! You wouldn't dare!"

Dare what? Kill myself? Jesus Christ, was that what she was thinking? These goddam nuns were really something. Didn't she realize that I was on that ledge out of a deep reverence for life? That I was trying to attach myself to the roof like a suction cup? That I was frozen solid? I wouldn't have jumped for a thousand bucks.

"Thomas! I forbid you! I absolutely forbid you to move a muscle. Stay right where you are. I'm going to get Father Grundy. He should see this. Then maybe he will understand what we go through." She pulled her head in. "Clara, you stay here and see that he doesn't move. Don't let any other children in. Band practice is canceled.

Mr. Clancy, go to my office and wait. You've caused enough trouble in here." Her head came out again. "You would be jumping right into the flames of Hell. I hope you realize that." Suicide was a sin. "You would be wrecking the school as well. Everything we have tried to build up."

I kept my mouth shut . . . for the simple reason that I couldn't open it. I could move my head a little and my eyes, but the rest of my body was like cold stone. My God, was I going to have to stand there forever like some kind of preposterous gargoyle?

3

Sister Mary Don Bosco must have wanted me to jump. She suggested it. I wasn't even considering it before she got there. She didn't ask me why I was on the ledge and she didn't ask me to come in. She only told me to stay there so that Father Grundy could see me go himself and not have to rely on her account of it. Maybe the strategy of the school was to identify troublemakers and then drive them out of the upper windows.

Well, I would not volunteer. They would have to use a crowbar on me. Father Grundy would have to lean out of the window and pry me off my perch. He would have to watch me fall rigidly away and drive myself headfirst into the ground like a stake, knowing he did it with his own hands.

Now that Sister had mentioned it, I *was* in an

ideal position to commit suicide. Standing on a ledge, it was more or less expected of you. If I didn't jump or at least threaten to, everybody would think I was crazy. Suicide is not all bad. It is, after all, a quick way to put an end to your problems. If I jumped I would get Hank in a lot of trouble because dozens of people saw him chasing me. That was a compensation. But I felt queasy in elevators; imagine how I would feel falling through the air. I'd probably throw up all the way to the ground.

MISUNDERSTOOD CATHOLIC YOUTH FROM GOOD FAMILY IN SPECTACULAR DEATH PLUNGE FROM ST. PROCOPIUS RAIN GUTTER

Old lady McLain, who lived alone in the bungalow across the street from us, would write one of her poems on her personalized blue stationery and take it all around the neighborhood making everybody read it.

TOMMY
What phantoms fought in this lad's head
That he should stand before us, dead?
Why did we lose this precious tot?
What did we do we shouldn't have ought?

("Very good, Mrs. McLain, very good indeed. You should send it in. I'd ask you for coffee, but I'm busy right now with the laundry and with things in the oven.")

If a person was going to end his life, I always

said, he should accomplish something by it, as Colin Kelly did when he dived his plane down that Japanese smokestack. He should turn himself over to medical students or try to reach some trapped miners. I didn't have any opportunities like that. I looked down at a teeter-totter. I could wait until somebody I hated sat down on the low side—like Mr. Spielmann, who aced my father out of the job of Street Commissioner. I could visualize him sitting down on the low side, straddling the board with his long legs and lighting a cigarette for a moment's rest. That's when I would come screaming out of the sky like a Kamikaze to spend my life against the high side, giving Mr. Spielmann a ride he would never forget.

"Tommy? Are you all right?" It was Sister Mary Jean, the nice nun, looking at me from the window. I certainly didn't want to upset her. She hadn't done anything.

"I'm okay," I said in a small voice. "I . . . I'm just looking at the view. You can see all the way to the steeple on Mount Sinsinawa from here."

"I'm afraid you might fall."

"So am I."

"Why did you go out there?"

"I was chased."

"Why don't you come in?"

"I can't move. Besides, Sister Don Bosco told me to wait here while she got Father Grundy."

"She told you to wait *there?*"

"That's right." I smiled a little. Having her there made me feel a lot better. I felt my muscles loosen slightly and I was able to turn my head to look at her. She leaned out of the window and stretched her hand toward me. It certainly was nice of her.

"Can you reach my hand?" she asked.

"I think so." The whole thing was embarrassing. I had scurried along that rain gutter at least fifty times from the fire escape to the window, now I was all tied up in knots—and right in front of Sister Mary Jean. My arm was like lead, but by putting all my effort into it and straining with all my might I was able to raise my hand to hers.

"I've got you!" she said, tightening her fingers around my wrist. She had a grip of steel! "Don't worry," she said. "You're okay now. Get down on your knees and crawl toward me."

I sank to my knees and edged myself along slowly. Now my arms and legs were beginning to feel rubbery, but before I knew it Sister's arm was around my shoulders and she was lifting me through the window. . . .

4

When Sister Don Bosco appeared with Father Grundy in tow and saw me inside the room she was mad. "I thought I told you to stay where you were," she said. "I gave you distinct orders not to move a muscle. Where is Clara Weems? I told her to stand guard."

"I asked her to leave," Sister Mary Jean said quietly. "I thought I would have a better chance

130

of getting Tommy to come in if nobody else was in the room."

"I don't recall delegating any such responsibility to you, Sister Mary Jean."

"I'm sorry. I did what I thought was best."

"What you thought was best was to defy my explicit instructions. What you don't seem to realize is that I have the entire school to think about. In my view it was important for the pastor of this parish to see with his own eyes the kind of willful disrespect that I as principal and you as a teacher have to put up with." She looked at me severely, for I was half to blame for coming in. "It appears that the opportunity is now lost."

"It's all right," said Father Grundy, stepping forward. "I can well imagine anything you might say about this fellow. I've had a great deal of trouble from him already."

"Well," said Sister Don Bosco, "I'm sorry I made you climb three flights of stairs for nothing."

"No harm done. As for whether it was proper for Sister Mary Jean to act without permission, I think that is a matter for later discussion between the two of you . . . I don't see that it concerns Thomas." He turned to me. "God will surely punish you for what you almost did when you stand before Him in judgment," he said in a carefully controlled voice. "But *we* must punish you as well, so you will never consider such a thing again. What more precious gift could God give you than life, yet you slapped Him in the face by threatening to end it. Do you realize the magnitude of your sin? Do you realize the scare you gave Sister Don Bosco? Do you realize what the news of this will do to your mother? I've known your mother and father for thirty years. They are good, hard-working people. They give hard-earned money for the support of this church and this school—not as much, perhaps, as they should, but a goodly amount nonetheless."

I looked at Sister Don Bosco. She didn't seem scared. She was nodding in full agreement with Father. Sister Mary Jean was agitated, trying not to interrupt.

"How dare you even think of jumping off that ledge?" Sister Don Bosco said. "You would have seriously befouled the reputation of St. Proco-pius. . . ."

"And you would have broken your mother's heart right smack in two," Father said, slapping his palms together smartly to emphasize his point, which made me jump in fright.

"But, I didn't . . . I wasn't . . . I wouldn't have . . . I didn't mean . . . ," I tried to say, beginning to cry.

"He wasn't going to jump," said Sister Mary Jean, at the end of her patience. "He was simply hiding out there. There is no point in badgering him over something he didn't intend to do."

"Is that true, Thomas?" asked Father Grundy, peering at me suspiciously.

"Y-Yes."

"Who were you hiding from? Who? Why?"

I looked desperately at Sister Mary Jean, but I

couldn't tell from her expression what she wanted me to say.

"Answer me!" demanded Father Grundy.

Hank was no friend of mine, but to rat on him was unthinkable. It would have made me an outcast to squeal on anybody, even under torture.

"What is the point of this?" Sister Mary Jean said, waving her arms. "Don't we all know he was trying to keep away from Henry Clancy, a boy twice his size, who chased him up here all the way from the street? I don't see how shouting at him will. . . ."

"Sister Mary Jean!" said Sister Don Bosco. "We have stood for all the interference from you that we are going to have stood for. Go to your room."

Sister Mary Jean took a deep breath, struggling to keep herself in check. "Sister Don Bosco. Father Grundy. Do me one favor. Give me one minute with you, alone. There." She pointed to the curtained doorway. "Tommy, you wait here for us." She walked to the curtain and waited.

The principal and the pastor glanced at each other, then followed her. Before they went behind the curtain, Father turned to me and said, "You leave this room and I'll thrash you within an inch of your life."

5

Jesus Christ, I could have saved everybody a lot of argument by just running across the room and swan-diving through the window. Instead, I decided to clean up the place. Maybe by playing the role of the good boy, the boy sorry for his sins, I could soften the blows that promised to rain on me. I started gathering the screens and piling them against the wall, but without trying to re-create a secret compartment. There would be time for that another day.

Father Grundy and the two nuns were talking in such strenuous whispers that I could hear most of what they were saying. As a matter of fact, I banged the screens together a little more than I had to so they wouldn't think I was listening.

Sister Don Bosco chewed out Sister Mary Jean, accusing her of an outrageous display of impertinence and insubordination, which bad as it would have been in any circumstances was ten times worse in front of a pupil. Father made soothing sounds to keep them from blowing up completely. According to Sister Don Bosco, Sister Mary Jean's violation of her vow of Obedience had been so flagrant that the Mother Superior at the priory in Wauseca, Wisconsin, would have to be consulted to determine the proper disciplinary action—action which, it wouldn't surprise Sister Don Bosco, might include a good long stint in the cloister. Father Grundy put in that as far as "the Shannon boy" was concerned, a harsh punishment would have to be administered to keep him in line, as that was the only language "his kind" could understand.

Sister Mary Jean countered vigorously. She said that assuming I was going to commit suicide was an incredible misreading of my personality, that I was mischievous but hardly insane, and that by ordering me to stay on the ledge instead of trying to coax me in Sister Don Bosco had exhibited such a dangerous lack of understanding that it was she, Sister Mary Jean, who was going to consult with the Mother Superior. Sister Don Bosco had courted disaster and created a crisis where none had existed, in the opinion of Sister Mary Jean. She told them that if I really were suicidal, harassment would only add to my motivation. She pointed out that I had been a completely normal boy at the beginning of the school year and that reporting this incident to my parents would merely show that St. Procopius could not deal with typical problems of adolescence, which could only add to the already high percentage of Catholic children enrolled in the public schools. Adding punishment on top of punishment was a clumsy, inquisitional approach to modern child psychology.

Sister Don Bosco said that two years at the state university had obviously addled Sister Mary Jean's mind beyond redemption, but Father Grundy said that they should stick to the problem at hand without getting involved in old arguments about secular education at the college level.

They calmed down after that and for five minutes they talked so softly I didn't catch a thing. When they reappeared they were models of composure. Father Grundy did the talking.

"Thomas," he said, "we have reached a decision. We feel that your flirtation with death and the near loss of your soul has taught you a lesson that we can't improve upon." He glanced around the room, noticing the way I had cleaned it up. "And because you seem to have the proper spirit of contrition, we will not punish you any further at this time."

What a break! Good old Sister Mary Jean!

"However," Father went on sternly, "you must make us a promise."

Oh-oh.

"You must promise never to go out on the ledge again and you must promise to do whatever your teachers tell you to do. Do you promise?"

"Yes, Father. Thank you, Father."

"Don't just say yes . . . make the whole promise."

"I promise not to go out on the ledge any more and I promise to do whatever my teachers tell me."

"Say that again looking at Sister Don Bosco instead of the floor."

I did, then returned my eyes to the floor. I waited to be dismissed.

"There is one more little matter," said Sister Don Bosco. "We might as well dispose of it now while we are together. This morning Sister Raphael intercepted a note Thomas had written. She didn't read it and I haven't had a chance to." She took it out of an inside pocket, still folded, and handed it to Father Grundy. "We should read it now so all the loose ends will be tied together. Father, you may have the honor." Sister Mary

Don Bosco looked pleased, while Sister Mary Jean frowned uneasily. I fell into a chair and buried my face in my hands. I should have jumped when I had the chance.

6

By raising my head and spreading my fingers I could watch the kindly pastor open my death certificate and smooth it flat on his palm. A weird, unearthly feeling came over me. I seemed to be looking at his hands from the far end of a long tunnel, and I no longer could feel the chair I was sitting on. Darkness pressed in around the edges of my vision and I had the distinct sensation that I was floating. Had I quietly died without a peep, just sitting there?

Father lowered the note and stared at me in puzzlement. "Why did you write this?"

I shrugged hopelessly. Unfortunately, I was still alive.

Sister Don Bosco took the paper from him. As she read the words her expression melted from triumph to confusion. Didn't they know what "rotten fuck" meant? Were they so otherworldly that they had never seen "fuck" before? Did I dare try to pretend that it meant something else? Let's see, if a fuck was a tropical fruit, then a rotten fuck. . . .

Sister Mary Jean took the note next, she who held me in such high esteem, she who had spoken up for me. Sorry, Sister Mary Jean. Boys get a bit dirty sometimes. It was nice being held in high esteem by you, even for a little while.

But she didn't react with shock and revulsion, either. She merely drew her eyebrows together and with a slight smile gave the paper to me. What the hell was going on? Had the writing become illegible, or what? No, the writing was legible, all right—it just wasn't mine. This was a different note entirely. In an approximation of my hand someone had scrawled, "Support our fighting men with your prayers."

"Why did you write that?" Father Grundy asked again. Was he trying to see if I would admit that it was not my note? I had only a split second to weigh my alternatives.

"I don't know," I said with a shrug. "Because I just figure they need all the help they can get."

"Why didn't you want Sister Raphael to read it?"

"Because I didn't want to look like a softy in front of my friends."

I braced myself, waiting for the jaws of a trap to spring shut on me, but nothing happened. There was an awkward silence. They knew I had a brother overseas. Finally Sister Don Bosco said, "All right, Thomas, you can go to class now."

Father stopped me at the door. "Thomas, I'll be hearing confessions starting at four o'clock. When school is out come to the church. I want to hear yours. I think this day might be a turning point in your life. You should wipe your slate clean."

"Yes, Father. Thank you, Father. Goodbye, Sister Mary Don Bosco. Goodbye, Sister Mary Jean."

"Goodbye, Thomas. God bless you."

CHAPTER NINE

1

I sat at my desk in a daze, confused about the note and filled with foreboding about having Father Grundy hear my confession. But what bothered me even more was the thought of how close I had come to killing myself out on the goddam rain gutter. It was somehow more real in retrospect than it was at the time. If I had lost my balance when my body was frozen stiff, I wouldn't have been able to save myself. When my legs turned rubbery just as Sister Mary Jean was hauling me in, I could easily have toppled over the edge and pulled her with me.

I wondered if I would have been given a full-scale Irish wake and funeral. Would they have staged a procession of my classmates carrying candles at a Requiem High Mass while Mrs. Hofstaeder coaxed tragic chords from the mighty organ? Would they toll the big bell in the steeple for me as they had for Monsignor McCauley, one baleful bong a minute for hours until all the Protestants in town were driven half out of their minds?

I pictured myself in an open coffin at the Wilcox and Ryan Funeral Home surrounded by decaying flowers while friends and relatives knelt briefly at my side, stealing glances at my artfully rouged and powdered face. (George Wilcox could have been an artist, everybody said. The job he did on Homer Kitchell after that car accident—Homer looked so *natural*.) I didn't look forward to dying and having Mr. Wilcox drain my blood, paint my lips, and exhibit me in Parlor A. If I had slipped off that ledge I would have tried to land face-first on something unyielding so that even Mr. Wilcox, with all his magic, would have had to accept a wake with a closed casket.

I dreaded my father's funeral, which I knew I would have to endure someday. He wasn't sick, but he couldn't last forever, not the way he drank and ate and not with the trouble he had with his piles. What made me worry about it was that I saw what Jimmy Kitchell went through when his dad got killed. Mr. Kitchell was the same age as my father. They were in World War I together. He even looked a little like my father—alive, that is. Dead he looked like hell, even though everybody at the wake told his wife, who stood drearily by the casket, that he looked wonderful, so peaceful, just as though he were sleeping. A lot of Irish people were at the wake, so naturally there was quite a bit of story-telling and hilarity. The laughter got so loud at one point that Mrs. Kitchell asked Mr. Wilcox to tell the men to quiet down, even though she knew they meant no disrespect and were only reacting to the tension.

At the cemetery crying was the problem, thanks to the American Legion. Just as Mr. Kitchell was being lowered into the grave and Father Grundy was sprinkling the casket with a handful of symbolic dirt, a red-faced man in a Legion uniform stepped out of the crowd, raised a trumpet to his lips, and played taps, very slowly. By the time he was done half the people were sobbing along with the immediate family of the deceased. When the wind carried the last lingering notes away through the trees and we thought we could get the hell out of there, another Legionnaire with a trumpet played taps from the top of the hill on the other side of the highway. Jesus, it was sad enough without that. The sound of taps echoing from a distant hilltop was more than anybody could stand, and the whole gathering broke down and blubbered. I cried a little myself and I didn't even like old man Kitchell.

For my father it would be ten times worse. Our family had lived in Dubuque for three generations and we had relatives beyond counting. My father's father had been a contractor, too, and between the two of them they had done work for every institution and business and in every neighborhood in a radius of fifty miles. A thousand people would show up at the cemetery for my father, and the Legion would probably post a trumpeter atop every bump in the county.

The Leonard E. Shannon Construction Co.
was pretty much a shoestring operation, long on
experience and know-how but short on capital
and machinery. Dad's entire equipment fleet con-
sisted of an old flatbed truck and a one-cylinder
concrete mixer. He bought a new car every two
or three years but quickly ruined it, much to my
mother's dismay, by using it for hauling. More
than once on Sunday morning we stopped in
front of Grandma McCleary's house to give her a
ride to Mass only to discover that the back seat,
where she was to sit, was loaded with picks, shovels, crowbars, trowels, and sacks of cement.

We could have been rich if my father had put
his mind to it, but he liked his euchre and his
highballs and his cronies at the Legion too much
for that. When a new job started he gave it his
full attention, working long hours and supervising every detail until he was sure the men knew
what had to be done and the cheapest way of
doing it. When the main problems had been
solved and things were moving along fairly
smoothly, his interest waned. Instead of submit-
ting bids on other jobs and in that way trying to
expand, he stayed a little later at the Legion at
night and slept a little later in the morning. By
the time the project was nearing completion he
was coming home at two or three in the morning,
his face flushed and his step unsteady. My

mother bawled him out unmercifully on those occasions, whatever the hour, showing a side to her personality that nobody outside the family suspected.

"That damned Legion and that dirty, rotten, stinking Arnold Gertz," my mother shouted at him, waking everybody. My brother and I would lie motionless in our beds, staring into the darkness, listening to her. "I slave all day to keep this house nice, cooking and washing and cleaning, and what do you do? You stay out half the night at that damned Legion playing cards and drinking with that dirty, rotten, stinking, filthy, rotten, drunken Arnold Gertz! I'm going to walk out of here someday and then you'll see how you like it. I'd be better off as a scrubwoman."

My father would never say a word. He sat on the edge of the bed, slowly took off his clothes, and put on his pajamas as if she weren't there. Finally my brother and I would hear the bed squeak as he lay down and we would see the slit of light under the door wink out. My mother usually carried on for a few minutes more, sometimes not stopping until she heard the regular sputtering of my father's snores.

"How much did you spend tonight?" she demanded rhetorically of the heap beside her. "Ten dollars? Twenty? While I struggle along with an icebox and a coal furnace and look like a damned fool in front of our friends? Oh, no, we can't afford anything for the house. Not a new rug in the parlor. The moth-eaten thing we have there now is good enough. No money for that. Because you are out all night spending every dime we've got with that damned Arnold Gertz at that dirty, rotten, filthy, stinking American Legion. You have a very bad case of piles and that damned fool of an Arnold Gertz knows it, yet he watches you pour the liquor down night after night. He ought to be shot."

When it was obvious that dad was asleep, the bed squeaked loudly as mom threw herself down and bounced about trying to get comfortable.

3

Things weren't as bad as she implied. We had enough to eat. Our household appliances were out-of-date but were in working order. My brother and I had bikes, sleds, and BB guns, and balls for every sport. The problem was that my father was indifferent to certain things my mother felt were of the highest significance, like rugs and dining room sets.

My father, all thing considered, was a good provider. When it came to food he was a terrific provider—especially of meat. To him, meat was basic. His theory seemed to be that as long as there was plenty of meat in the house nobody had any reason to complain about anything. Before meat rationing was imposed—a drastic measure that brought home to my father the importance of winning the war quickly—it was a scandal the meat my mother had to throw out. She begged him not to bring home so much, but he couldn't

146

help himself. Sometimes he came home in the middle of the day after a visit to Winkler's Meat Market with his arms full of little packages wrapped in brown butcher paper, which he would pour onto the kitchen table.

"Oh, *no*," my mother would say, "not more meat. . . ."

But it would be more meat: spare ribs, short ribs, chipped beef, corned beef, roast beef, stew beef, ground beef, beef jerky, and turkey. The next day it might be bacon, baloney, salami, pastrami, bratwurst, knockwurst, liverwurst, and squab.

"Leonard, stop buying so much meat. The icebox is full of meat. I'll just have to throw it out or give it away. . . ."

Lamb shanks, lamb chops, veal shanks, veal chops, chuck roast, pot roast, pork roast, pork chops, leg of lamb, rack of lamb, sweetbreads, and crab.

"You simply must stop bringing home all this meat, Leonard. Winkler's must think we have fifty deserters hiding in the attic. We have enough meat for a month. No more meat until I say so, understand?"

Capons and cutlets, pullets and mullets. He didn't care much for fish, so on Friday he hardly ate at all, which gave my mother a breathing spell. My father claimed that the Church's fish-on-Friday rule had been pushed through by the Twelve Apostles, who were fishermen by trade. On Saturday, though, he swung into action again and bumped the kitchen door open with an armload of baked ham, boiled ham, smoked ham, ham hocks, knuckles, briskets, and liver.

"Leonard, this is going too far. We have no more room for meat. The icebox is jammed full. I can't put meat in the closets and under the beds. I'm going to call Winkler's and tell them not to sell you any more. Please! No more meat. We have enough meat. Don't bring any more meat home. Please!"

Salisbury steak, porterhouse steak, T-bone steak, minute steak, market steak, hasenpfeffer, Swiss steak, ground steak, round steak, chuck steak, shank steak, flank steak, plank steak. . . .

4

When the bell rang ending afternoon recess, I was walking up the stairs with Roger, telling him about my adventures in the Band Room and how the note turned out to be the wrong one.

"Hey," he said, a light bulb flashing above his head. "I think I saw somebody grab that note off Sister's desk. . . ."

"What? Who? When? How?"

He thought hard. "I think it was Ellen Ettelsly. Yeah, it must have been her . . . she sits right next to it. I just sort of saw an arm reach out."

"She couldn't have. You must be nuts. I had my eyes glued on that note all the time."

"Not while Sister was clobbering Elbows, I'll bet. Everybody was watching the action. That's when I saw something out of the corner of my eye. I remembered it just now when you were talking. I'm almost sure it was Ellen."

"Naw, you must be nuts," I said. "Jesus, not Ellen. Christ, anybody but her. I can't believe it. She's the biggest suck in school. Oh, Jesus Christ."

All through civics I stared at Ellen, trying to read her mind or get a clue. She didn't glance in my direction until we were told to get out our history books. With her desk top raised she turned her head and looked right at me.

With elaborate pantomime I mouthed the words, "Do you have the note?"

She looked away without answering and almost without changing her expression, but I was sure I detected a hint on her face that showed she *knew something*. There was a trace of a smile, as if she were relishing my anguish. Well, I'll be goddammed. Was it possible that Ellen Ettelsly had switched the notes, thereby saving my ass? She had never shown the slightest interest in me and I had never given her any reason to. Did she have secret hotpants for me? It was incredible, but it would have been just my luck. The only girls who liked me at all were jokes like Bernice Vorwald, who weighed in at two hundred and ten, and dumb Constance Overmyer, whose tits were like two peas on a board. The girls I was hot for shunned me like a leper. Ellen was neutral—zero on the Colgate Laugh Meter—although she was far from ugly. Was it my destiny to lose my cherry to the class brain?

The rest of the afternoon was agonizingly long.

I kept my nose in a book and ignored all signals from my helpful friends to turn around and get into a little extra trouble. Elbows, Roger, and Kites—some friends.

5

"Ellen! Ellen!" I spotted her two blocks from school, just before she got to her house. She looked back but didn't stop walking. "Whew . . . hi . . . excuse me . . . ," I said breathlessly, catching up to her. "Hey, Ellen, there's something I've got to know . . . whew! . . . about the note . . . did you . . I mean somebody said you . . . the note Sister took from me . . . did you . . . ?"

She looked at me without pity, shaking her head as if I were a pretty sad excuse for a human being. "Yes," she said, "I have your note. Here. . . ." She handed it to me, still in a wad.

"Oh, gee, thanks. Thanks a lot. You really saved my life. Gee, Ellen, I'm sorry about what I wrote. I sure didn't mean it. I was just trying to be funny."

"I didn't read it."

"You didn't? You didn't read it?"

"No. I thought it would be disgusting, so I didn't."

"But then, why did you . . . I mean, if you didn't want to . . . ?"

"I took it because I didn't want Sister to read it, and I put another one in its place so she wouldn't suspect anything. You got so excited when she grabbed it I was sure it was filthy. It's just not right that a nun should have to see things like that. Really, it's terrible the way you boys treat her. You are just as bad as the rest, Tommy Shannon. She's not perfect, but she does the best she can."

"Well, she doesn't treat us so hot, either," I reminded her. "I've been hit by her every single day this year. How do you think I like that? I don't like that at all."

"I said she wasn't perfect. I hate it when she hits people. I actually get sick to my stomach. And I knew if she read that note there would be some more hitting. I don't believe in people hitting people. My gosh, if we can't get along with each other at St. Procopius, is it any wonder that there is so much shooting going on in the world?"

I had to hand it to her. She not only got straight A's, she kept up on world affairs, too. We had arrived at her front door and when she told me she was going inside I found myself wanting her not to. Ellen Ettelsly! Good God, what was ailing me? She wasn't sexy at all. Or was she? Her face was pretty nice, especially her mouth, which was like a valentine, but she was too thin. Of course, so was I. There was something different about her, though, not just that she was smart. She wasn't giggly and nervous like the other girls. She didn't seem to be afraid of me. Most of the girls were scared of the boys, but not Ellen. Jesus Christ, she was looking me right in the eye and bawling the hell out of me. It took nerve to switch those notes. She plainly had qualities nobody had noticed.

"Ellen, have you got a date for the graduation dance?" What the hell, I might as well ask her. The girls with conspicuous boobs already had dates and the more I looked at Ellen the more I wanted to go with her instead of hanging around on a street corner somewhere with Kites and Roger and Elbows. With Ellen I could at least have an adult conversation. Not only that, by taking her out a few times now I would be making an investment that could pay handsome dividends later in high school, when she might fill out.

"Why?" she asked.

"I mean, do you have a date? Are you going with anybody?"

"Why do you want to know?"

She was tough. I would have to commit myself. "Because I'd like to take you. If you don't have a date. Do you?"

"I don't know."

"You don't know?"

"I'll tell you tomorrow."

"Well, okay. I'll see you tomorrow. I've got to go to confession now." I thought I would throw that in to imply that I was holy, hence harmless.

Walking toward the church I thought about how the guys would laugh when I showed up at the dance with Ellen Ettelsly. But they wouldn't laugh so much when I told them that it was Ellen who had the guts to switch the notes while they all sat around with their thumbs up their asses. She wasn't the teacher's pet everybody thought she was. One thing worried me, though. I had talked to her for ten minutes without getting an erection. Did that mean she would one day be my wife, just as my mother wanted?

CHAPTER TEN

1

It would be nice to have a date for the graduation dance. I remembered the Christmas party, which Kites, Roger, Elbows, and I didn't go to because we thought it was for sissies. The four of us hid in the parking lot across from the church making snowballs to throw at the kids when they came out and hopping from one foot to the other to keep warm. To pass the time we tried to figure out how many miles of pipe were laid every night in the bedrooms of the world. We estimated that there were five hundred million couples between the ages of puberty and senescence that slept together. If they screwed once every ten days, if the average stroke was four inches long, and if it took thirty strokes to reach orgasm, then there were ten feet of pipe laid per couple every ten days, or *five hundred million feet* every night! That's a lot of pipe. In miles it's one hundred thousand, or halfway to the moon, *every night*. The four of us were still looking forward to our first inch.

Such calculations get boring after a time, especially when the temperature is below freezing. It finally got so late and so cold that we went home without throwing a single snowball. Before leaving, though, we did write some dirty words in the snow with piss.

I wondered if I would get a hard-on dancing with Ellen. There wasn't much chance of it happening under the watchful eyes of the nuns, who would be sitting along one wall of the church basement, or with Father Grundy, who would be doing his duty with a twelve-inch ruler. Father kept his eyes peeled for couples dancing too close. When he spotted one he charged across the floor and thrust his ruler between them. Twelve inches, in his estimation, was the minimum safe distance. No, the problem would come later, when a group of us adjourned to someone's house for cheek-to-cheek dancing. If Ellen had perfume on, if my nose was in her hair, if it was too dark to see her clearly, I would almost certainly become tumescent, I don't care if she was a bit bony. Should I back up so she couldn't feel me, or should I be a man and press myself against her? I knew what would happen if I was dancing cheek-to-cheek with Ellen Ettelsly, or anybody, and I got an erection, and she let me press it against her. I would go home with a splotch on my pants.

I pulled open one of the huge double doors of the church and went inside, dipping my middle finger in the bowl of Holy Water and blessing myself. I genuflected in the aisle and slipped into

156

a rear pew, kneeling down for an Examination of Conscience before going into the confessional.

The church was cavernous and gloomy. The tops of the varnished pews stretched away from me like the brown surface of Rafferty's Slough at sunset. In the far corner, in front of the statue of the Blessed Virgin, an old woman was lighting Vigil Candles and dropping coins into the metal box. Each time she lit a candle for a special intention she had to drop a quarter in the slot, even though she could have gotten three candles that size for a dime at Kresge's. But I don't want to get into that.

The altar light was burning behind its pane of red glass, suspended from a chain that rose all the way to the highest part of the vaulted ceiling, so I knew that the Blessed Eucharist was behind the little golden doors of the tabernacle. God was present; you could feel it. Brother Bartholomew said he could go into any Catholic church blindfolded and tell whether or not the Blessed Eucharist was in the tabernacle or exposed to view in a Monstrance. When the Eucharist wasn't there, he said, the church was nothing but a big room, but when the altar light was on it was the house of God and you could sense His living presence. This point bothered me because we were told that God was everywhere at all times. So how could He be gone when the Eucharist wasn't there?

There were a lot of tricky problems like that connected with being a Catholic, problems that made Catholicism so vastly superior to other religions. By having to do a little work and by having your faith tested once in a while you made yourself worthy to enter the Kingdom of God. Other religions were so easy that they didn't make you eligible for any reward when you died.

Take the matter of foreknowledge and foreordination, which was explained to us one Sunday in a sermon by a visiting monk whose name I can't recall. Just because God knows what is going to happen in advance doesn't mean He makes it happen, which would be foreordination and which would leave free will rather up in the air. Man is free to change his mind. God knows which choice man will make in the exercise of his free will, but that is not the same thing as saying God forces him to make it, even though God could have constructed man in such a way that his free will could have led him to make some other choice, which God also would have anticipated. This was an elusive concept, and once understood was easily forgotten, like the infield fly rule.

The Blessed Trinity was troublesome, too. There is only one God: God the Father, God the Son, and God the Holy Ghost. Each is a separate and distinct part of an indivisible whole. Belief in more than one God is the pagan sin of polytheism, which you had to be careful to avoid when praying to the various persons of the Trinity and to the various saints who had special powers of intercession with this one or that one.

The Virgin Mary is a good one to pray to for help because she naturally occupies a very high position in the eyes of God the Father, who chose her, God the Son, who was born to her, and God the Holy Ghost, who got her with child. Actually, since Mary is the mother of the Son of God, she is the Mother of God, the Wife of God and God Herself, all at the same time, as well as being a virgin.

2

Kneeling in church thinking about these matters and thinking about Ellen reminded me that she had once gotten into trouble by asking too many questions in religion class. If you will open your missal to the Canon, just before the Consecration, you will note that there is a place for the priest to mention the names of people for whom the Mass is being said. You could have a Mass said for anybody for a donation of a dollar. Five dollars got you a High Mass, complete with Sister Valeriamina's Upper Class Mixed Choir and Father Grundy in his most expensive vestments. The persons mentioned benefited greatly; if they were living they might get divine assistance on a worthy intention, and if they were dead they might get some time lopped off their sentences in Purgatory. This might sound like the same buying of indulgences that led to the Diet of Worms in 1521, but it wasn't that at all. The donations were simply a means of defraying the expenses of candles, incense, and electricity, which didn't come free even to the One, True Church.

What Ellen asked about was the exact amount

159

of grace or indulgence the people got who were named by the priest during Mass. Sister Raphael answered that God had never revealed that information, but that it was a lot.

"Does each person get less the more names are mentioned?"

"No," said Sister Raphael. "Each one gets just as much as if he had been mentioned alone."

"Then why," Ellen persisted, "doesn't the priest dedicate the Mass to everybody, living and dead, instead of just a few? There must be lots of dead people who are very deserving but who don't have any friends left to have Masses said for them. It doesn't seem fair."

It was a tough question and it made Sister nervous. She told Ellen to stay after school. If I had asked a question like that she would have told me that I would understand when I was older or that it was one of the Mysteries that came with the gift of faith, and let it go at that. But such a question coming from Ellen, who was taken for granted as a devout believer, upset Sister Raphael, who apparently feared that Ellen had been touched by Doubt, which, if not countered at once, might lead her down the dark pathway that ended in atheism and syphilis. She had to go to private counseling sessions with Father Grundy every night for a week.

The rest of us learned an important lesson: It didn't pay to ask certain kinds of questions. Besides, it was silly to expect comprehensible answers to questions that giant minds like St. Augustine had grappled with for a lifetime before

160

understanding. We would never be smart enough to follow his reasoning, so why try? Why not accept his conclusions? He was one of the holiest and most brilliant men who ever lived and his word was good enough for us.

Some of the guys gave Ellen a hard time for having to go to extra religion classes. When they passed her in the hall they would hiss, "Atheist," just loud enough for her to hear, which made her cry. I never teased her though; her family and mine were too friendly.

Examining my conscience before going to confession, I realized what a bonanza it might be if Ellen really were an atheist. An atheist didn't believe in God, and what is more important, probably didn't believe in Hell, either. If she didn't believe in Hell, then she might not have any particular objection to lying down and letting me. . . .

. . . Which was a foolish line of thought to pursue because I would just have to confess it. Banging a girl in your mind was considered just as sinful as banging her in your bed, believe it or not. The guy who enjoyed all the fun of really screwing a girl was no worse off than the poor sonofabitch who only dreamed about it. How do you like that? Have you ever heard of anything more ridiculous? I got so mad thinking about it that I squirmed in my pew and cursed under my breath. It was the dumbest, most unfair law in the whole world. And do you know who was responsible for it? That goddam St. Augustine, that's who.

It was not very reasonable of me to suppose that Ellen Ettelsly was ever going to hook a finger in my collar and pull me down on top of her. She was too skinny to get that hot for anybody. In my fantasies only girls with round, full bodies got so crazed with lust that they tore at my clothes.

Getting to first base with Ellen was going to be a long, hard struggle. It would take six dates at least before she would let me hold her hand, six more before a kiss goodnight, six more before a necking session, six necks—each of which would leave me with splotched pants—before I would dare try to touch her small but not inconsequential boobs. Beyond that I couldn't project.

3

I settled down to the business of examining my conscience, sorting out the dark deeds and thoughts that I would have to tell Father Grundy. To get myself in the mood I silently recited the Confiteor.

I confess to almighty God, to
blessed Mary, ever virgin, to blessed
Michael the archangel, to blessed
John the Baptist, to the holy apostles,
Peter and Paul, to all the saints, and
to you, Father, that I have sinned
exceedingly in thought, word and deed,
through my fault, through my fault,

through my most grievous fault. Therefore
I beseech blessed Mary, ever virgin,
blessed Michael the archangel, blessed
John the Baptist, the holy apostles,
Peter and Paul, and you, Father,
to pray to the Lord our God for me.

In my opinion, most of the things I had done
since my last confession were only venial and not
mortal sins, which is to say that if I had dropped
dead at that moment I would have gone to Purgatory for a while instead of being stuck forever in
Hell. Not that Purgatory was a bargain. It was
every bit as hot as Hell, but you stayed there only
until your soul was purified by the flames. How
long it took to burn off various kinds of venial
sins was unknown. That a great deal of time was
required was obvious from the size of the indulgences attached to the saying of certain prayers. I
wore a medal around my neck that depicted the
Holy Family with these words: "Jesus, Mary and
Joseph! Hear the prayer of thy servant! 300 days
each time. Copyright 1934 by the Ablutionist Fathers." Every time you said that prayer you spent
three hundred fewer days in Purgatory. So the
sentences meted out for venial sins were appall-
ingly huge, at least in the opinion of the Ablutionist Fathers.

It was enough to make you envy the Hindus,
who had not yet received the Gospel. Hindus
could screw day and night without a worry in the
world because they didn't know any better. If
they died while still in their ignorant state they

would go to Limbo. Limbo, Monsignor McCauley told us before he croaked, was just as nice as heaven with one exception—the souls there never saw God. That didn't seem like enough punishment to me. Of course, they would have to spend eternity with infants who had died at birth and with uneducated people from the Stone Age who weren't around when Christ brought the gift of Baptism.

Baptism not only washes the stain of Original Sin off your soul, but every other sin as well. Unfortunately, you can only be baptized once. Catholics are baptized when they are only a few weeks old, long before they have the coordination to commit any sins. That's nice for kids who cry themselves to death during the ceremony and who are relaxing in heaven today, but it is a disservice to those who survive into junior high school. My friends and I often daydreamed about how nice it would be not to have been baptized. Then we could pillage and rape freely, knowing that when death approached a priest would baptize us, after which our souls would be as pure as the driven snow, ready to ascend into heaven and be happy with God for ever and ever.

But with my luck I would have been struck by lightning coming out of a whorehouse. In Hell nobody listens to explanations. That's why I went to confession every month or so; it was too risky not to. Going to confession was hard, but the feeling afterward was wonderful. Afterward I felt clean and fresh and pure. I was angelic for a day or two, resisting lewd thoughts, keeping my paws off my pudendum except for purposes of bodily elimination, and saying hello to old people. It was nice knowing that a tragic accident would send me straight to heaven.

4

The confession box was like three Gothic phone booths. Behind the middle door sat the priest, hearing first the confession of the penitent on one side, then the one on the other. I waited in line for a while until the compartment on the left was empty. I went inside, shut the door, and knelt down. It was very dark but there was enough light filtering through the pane of frosted glass that I could make out the outline of the linen handkerchief that covered the sliding panel in the partition between the priest and me. It was so quiet that I could hear the whispers of the woman in the other booth, who must have been hard of hearing. It would have been a sin to eavesdrop, so I blotted out the sound by rubbing my palms back and forth on my ears.

I almost never went to confession at St. Procopius. It was much easier psychologically to go in a different parish, where the priest didn't know you. When you had to tell a priest that you had pressed your organ against Darlene Hollenback's hip for twelve blocks on a crowded bus, you didn't want to have to look him in the eye the next day. Once when I had shot my wad French-kissing somebody, I bicycled all the way to St.

Boniface's because I was sure nobody there knew me. When I was leaving the confessional, the priest—I still don't know who he was—said, "Say, Tommy, would you open a window before you go?" Since then I have expected every priest I have ever met to call me aside and tell me what a disgusting thing it was that I did to that girl with my tongue.

The door of the other booth opened and closed. Father Grundy's chair squeaked as he turned toward me and opened the sliding panel. A square of dim light appeared in the center of the handkerchief, which framed the shadowy profile of his face. "Go ahead," he whispered.

"Confiteor Deo omnipotenti, beatae Mariae semper virgini, beato Michaeli archangelo . . ." nothing like a recitation of the Confiteor in Latin to disarm a confessor . . . *"beato Joanni Baptistae, sanctis apostolis Petro et Paulo . . ."*

"There's no need to . . . ," Father tried to say.

". . . omnibus sanctus, et tibi Pater, quia peccavi nimis cogitatione. . . ."

"Very good, but would you mind skipping ahead to . . ."

". . . verbo et opere: mea culpa, mea culpa, mea maxima culpa. Ideo precor beatam Mariam semper virginem . . ."

"This is Tommy, isn't it?"

". . . beatum Michaelem archangelum, beatum Joannem Baptistam . . ."

"I thought so."

". . . santos Apostolos Petrum et Paulum,

omnes sanctos et te, Pater, orare pro me ad Dom-
inum Deum nostrum."

"Yes. Well. That wasn't necessary. Suppose you get right to your confession."

"Bless me, Father, for I have sinned," I said as softly as I could, using the words I had been taught in the second grade and not bothering to disguise my voice. "It has been four weeks since my last confession and I have committed the following sins. I missed my morning prayers three times, I disobeyed my father and mother twice, I used God's name in vain four times, I masturbated eight times, and I had evil thoughts a hundred and nineteen times. I am sincerely sorry for having committed these sins and promise never to commit them again."

"Fine. Hmm. Now, Thomas, you must pray to God to help you overcome temptations of the flesh. Imagine the Christ-child and His Blessed Mother and the tears that stream down Their holy faces when you abuse the body God has given you and when you allow impure thoughts to invade your mind. When these temptations arise pray to God to give you the strength to cast them aside. You can become a splendid example in the eyes of God, your family, and Holy Mother Church of a Christian youth, whose head is high and whose eyes are clear, who doesn't have to slink through life ashamed and debased by the carnal evil of self-pollution. Do you understand, Thomas? Do you understand that from this day forward you must march forward with a pure heart and a pure mind, strong in God's love, Who died for your sins?"

"Yes, Father."

"Did you make a complete confession?"

"Yes, Father."

"You have not lost your temper, or received Communion sacrilegiously, or harbored any doubts about the laws of God or God's Church?"

"No, Father."

"You have not been jealous, obstinate, or slothful?"

"No, Father."

"You have not touched anyone impurely?"

"You mean ever, or since my last confession?"

"Since your last confession."

"No, Father." Then I thought of crumping. I had crumped a few guys. Crumping a guy in the crotch with the back of your hand wasn't done for sexual excitement—it was simply a test of alertness and reflexes. Mainly, it was a way for big guys to humiliate little guys. But a priest might consider it an impure touch, so I thought I better change my answer. "I mean, yes, Father, I guess I have."

His voice perked up. "You have indulged in impure touches? Of the genital region?"

"Well . . . yes."

"Why didn't you confess it?"

"I just now thought of it."

"Did you engage in these acts on more than one occasion?"

"Yes, Father."

"With the same person?"

168

"No, with various different persons."

"I see. Were these girls Catholic or non-Catholic?"

"They weren't girls, Father. . . ."

"You mean they were boys?"

"Yes. What we do is. . . ."

"You . . . you have been engaging in homosexual practices with other boys?" He was getting excited, abandoning his whispers.

"It just takes a second with each one, Father. It's not really. . . ."

"Here at St. Procopius?"

"Yes, Father, but. . . ."

"In the boys' room?"

"No, usually just in the hallways or anywhere."

"God in heaven have mercy on our souls! How many times?"

"You mean that I did it, or had it done to me?"

"I don't care! God help us! That you did it!"

"Since my last confession?"

"Yes!" He was practically shouting—everybody in the church could hear him.

"I don't know, maybe twenty times . . . but not nearly as many times as the other guys. . . ."

"*What!?*" There was a loud banging and bumping as he jumped to his feet and began turning around, knocking over his chair and falling against the walls of his cubicle in a very disoriented fashion. I don't know what he was doing—maybe trying to get hold of the doorknob to get out of there. Apparently he was under the impression that his entire school from kindergar-

169

ten up had become infested with fuzzy-faced fruits.

"Father," I hissed into the handkerchief, "you have the wrong idea . . . it's not what you are thinking."

He righted his chair and collapsed on it with a thud. I could hear his loud breathing. After he had settled down a little he leaned toward me and whispered in a voice that trembled with emotion. "This is the most outrageous, monstrous. . . ."

"Father, listen. I didn't actually touch anybody the way you think, and nobody touched me. I'm no queer. There aren't any queers in school that I know about. I don't even know what a queer looks like. All we do is sort of flick our hands at a person's, well, ah, organs as we walk by, just to kind of keep him on his toes. There isn't anything arousing about it. Just the opposite."

He didn't know what the hell I was talking about, so I explained it again. I explained it five times before I was through, using different words each time so that he would understand. He finally did, and he even thanked me for telling him about it. Apparently nobody else ever had. He said it was a disgusting, filthy practice that was definitely sinful as well as dangerous and that he would take steps to put a stop to it, which I said would be fine with me. I told him I hated it, which was the truth. My throat was hurting from all the whispering.

"All right," he said. "Are you sorry for the sins you have committed?"

"Yes, Father."

"Then make a good Act of Contrition."

He mumbled the prayer of Absolution in his usual slurred Latin while I recited the formula prescribed for me: "Oh my God I am heartily sorry for having offended Thee, and I detest all my sins, because I dread the loss of Heaven and the pains of Hell, but most of all because I have offended Thee, my God, Who art all good and deserving of all my love. I firmly resolve, with the help of Thy grace, to confess my sins, to do penance, and to amend my life, amen."

The shadow of his hand blessed me. "I absolve thee in the name of the Father, the Son, and the Holy Ghost. Go in peace and say a prayer for me."

"Father! My penance . . . you forgot to give me a penance."

"Oh. Three Our Fathers and three Hail Marys." He slammed shut the sliding panel.

He must have made a mistake. I expected something far worse, like a rosary for each of the Twelve Promises to St. Margaret Mary, but I didn't intend to wait around for him to change his mind. I must have been in that confessional for twenty minutes, and it was like an oven.

When I came out the people who were waiting in line glared at me as if I were Oscar Wilde or somebody. I usually knelt down and got my penance out of the way immediately, but not that day. I couldn't take those looks. I beat it out the front door.

5

On the way home I met Willie Richards. I was dying to tell somebody about what happened to me in the confessional, but not him. As a Protestant he wouldn't have understood, and I didn't feel like getting into a big discussion of the sacraments.

"Where have you been lately, Willie?" I asked, trying to fall in with his longer strides. "Don't you go out at night any more? We've been having a great time."

"Maybe I'll see you tonight," he said. "It'll probably be more interesting than finger-fucking Wanda Farney again."

"What?"

"I said I get tired of finger-fucking Wanda Farney all the time."

"What sort of shit is this you're trying to feed me?"

"I'm not shitting you. I've been in her pants every night for two weeks."

"Two weeks, huh? Then how come you're not telling me about it until now?"

"Because I thought I was hot for her at first. Now I don't think I am, so I'm telling you. Besides, it's getting boring. It's all she'll let me do. I can't even feel her tits, for chrissakes. She says she's saving that for her husband."

Willie Richards was very clean-cut looking and if you didn't know him you wouldn't believe he could commit a venial sin, much less a mortal one. But with Wanda Farney? Jesus Christ, I thought to myself, that takes the cake. I sit three seats from her every day and she always looks so innocent and stupid. Wanda Farney, who wouldn't even let me so much as kiss her on the cheek after taking her to two movies—now she's letting Willie Richards finger-fuck her night after night, and he's not even a Catholic. Shit.

"It's funny," he said matter-of-factly, "she won't neck on a sofa or in a car or on the grass. Only standing up on her front porch. That's the only time I get any place. With her folks right inside the door listening to the radio. I kiss her good night and I back her against the wall and I press my knee against her snatch and pretty soon I'm in. This finger." He held up the middle finger of his right hand. "This is the finger right here."

I grimaced and shook my head. I felt myself hating that conceited Protestant sonofabitch, fooling around with a Catholic girl like that, telling me about it right after Confession when I was in a state of grace.

"You better cut that stuff out, Willie," I said. "You can get all kinds of terrible diseases. Not only that, it's a mortal sin to gain carnal knowledge of a woman. If you died right now you would go straight to Hell."

"Bullshit."

"Bullshit, my ass. It's the truth." In the back of my mind I was wondering if I could get out of my date with Ellen, if she said yes the next day, and get one with Wanda instead. I wasn't as handsome or confident as Willie Richards, but maybe now that he had broken through her defenses and told me how to do it she would be a pushover for me as well. If I could get up enough nerve to back her against the wall, maybe she would go to pieces and grab my hand and. . . . But first I had to get Willie out of the picture.

"Hell is terrible," I told him. "It's solid flames. All you can hear are the screams of the people around you and you can smell the burning flesh. You can feel the pain as your ears and eyelids burn off. . . ."

"Bullshit. Just for playing stinkfinger with Wanda Farney? Don't make me laugh."

"You won't laugh when you die. You'll be in Hell and you won't get out. It's not like Purgatory. And it's not like Limbo either."

"You Catholics are nuts. You talk as if I was screwing her or something."

"But it *is* like you were screwing her. If she closes her eyes she probably thinks you *are* screwing her. Does she close her eyes?"

"She closes her eyes for everything, even holding hands. I was walking down the sidewalk with her holding hands and she ran right into a fucking fireplug."

"This isn't funny! I'm worried about you. Hell is horrible and I don't want any friend of mine winding up there. God knows how to punish people."

"What's gotten into you, anyway, Tommy? You are always as horny as the next guy, and now all of a sudden you're giving me all this God shit."

"I've been doing some serious thinking."

"Well, quit it. I'm never going to tell you another thing." We walked along in silence for a moment. Then he said, "Hell couldn't be like you say. If you were dead you couldn't feel the fire."

"That's where you are wrong," I shot back. "God brings you to life so you can feel the pain, and He keeps you alive so you can keep feeling it."

"I don't believe it. God's not going to stop running the solar system because of what I do with my middle finger. This finger right here." He held the goddam thing up again.

"Like hell He won't," I said. "It's your immortal soul you are fooling around with, you know. You should read what St. Augustine went through just for stealing an apple. He reached over a fence and took an apple, and then for days afterward he was in agony over it, thinking of what a terrible thing he had done. He knew how dirty he was in the eyes of God. And all he did was steal an apple, not finger-fuck his girl friend."

"But he was a *saint*, for chrissakes. I'm not going to be a saint. I'm going to be a pharmacist."

We had arrived at my house. "I'm trying to do you a favor," I said with heat. "Stop seeing Wanda! Stop while you still can! Do you pull down her pants or do you just sort of slip your hand underneath?"

Willie looked at me with sudden understanding. "So that's it!" he said, beginning to smile. "You want her for yourself! Well, why didn't you say so? I've got plenty of other girls. You want Wanda? Take her."

"Jesus, Willie, do you really mean it?"

"Sure I do. I'm tired of her. She's all yours. Good luck. Just sort of slip your hand underneath."

"Jesus Christ, thanks a lot."

"Forget it."

CHAPTER ELEVEN

1

June 5, 1944

Dear Mom and Dad and Tommy:

I'll see you in two weeks! Yes, now that we've got the war won they figure it's safe to let me take a little trip to the old home town. When I get to Chicago I'll call you and tell you which train to meet. Those cornfields will sure look good!

The Italians didn't put up much of a fight, did they? But the————are still fighting like————. But we've just about got them now.

Stock up on fresh eggs and Winkler's veal sausage and fresh milk—that's what I'm going to want every morning. Anyone caught serving powdered milk or powdered eggs gets shot on sight!

There is something I've got to tell you. I've got crutches. I thought I better tell you so there won't be a big commotion when you see them. Hear that, Ma? It's nothing to worry about and I don't want a lot of carrying on when I get off the train.

How does Tommy feel about graduating from eighth grade? Is he ready for high school? Tell him to work on his hook shot, because a hook shot is almost impossible to block.

See you soon! (It sure feels good to write that!)

Your son,
Paul

As you might guess, my mother cried when she read this letter. My father put his arm around her. "He's coming home," he said, "that's the main thing. The crutches are probably because of his foot. The Army is very careful about feet— they want them to heal up right. And don't worry about getting the sausage . . . I'll get the sausage. Come on, don't cry. I'm sure if he was hurt bad he would have told us."

Which is exactly what my mother wasn't sure of. Paul hadn't mentioned his foot at all in his last couple of letters; now the news about the crutches.

"He'll probably have the Purple Heart," I said, trying to help dad console her. "Won't that be terrific? He'll be able to marry anybody in town, and get any job he wants. And wait till he sees my hook shot! He'll really be surprised. . . ."

She quit crying eventually, but not before saying a rosary and doing the supper dishes. By the time I left the house she had pretty much gotten over the shock of hearing about the crutches and was on the phone telling her friends the good news that Paul was coming home at last.

The guys in the gang were just as happy about it as I was. Like me, they could hardly wait to question him about combat and hear some thrilling stories about our victories over the dirty Germans. In my honor Porky decided that we should break the streetlight in front of the police station and that I should be allowed to throw the rock. I thanked him for his faith in me and vowed that my rock would be the only one needed.

That particular streetlight was one we had never dared attack before, not just because it was in front of the police station but because it was on a downtown street far from the golf course and without hiding places. But Porky had been working on the problem and had come up with a plan worthy of the French underground. We made our approach and getaway through a storm drain that ran from the harbor, where Mule Kahlback waited in his car, to a manhole in the middle of the street under the light. Porky lifted the manhole cover a few inches with the top of his head to make sure nobody was around, then pushed it to one side so I could climb out with my rock.

I imagined the light as a German flare floating over a no-man's land where my brother, wounded in the foot, was dragging himself across barbed wire and craters toward the safety of Allied lines. The Nazi machine-gunners spotted him and swung their muzzles around, but before the deadly chatter could begin I leaped to my feet and threw my grenade upward into the night sky . . . bull's-eye! There was a resounding smashing of glass and some flashes of electric sparks as the battlefield was plunged into blackness.

"Nice shot," Porky whispered as I squeezed past him down the ladder. He pulled the heavy lid back onto its seat, pausing for a moment to enjoy the sounds of the cops rushing out of the station, searching for commandos that seemed to be invisible. We went down the ladder to the bottom and turned on our flashlights. Running two blocks through a four-foot-high pipe wasn't hard when you knew that you had once again foiled the enemy and saved your brother from harm.

Porky seemed to be changing, willing to lead us into taking greater and greater risks. News of battlefield victories were in the papers almost every day, and they seemed to make him nervous, as if he were running out of time before he could enlist. He apparently wanted to establish a reputation as a military expert before he was even in the army. He had begun to borrow his father's car because, he said, the enemy might recognize Mule's. We didn't know at the time that Porky had to push the car down his driveway with the lights and engine off so his father wouldn't know it was gone.

At Porky's urging we had burned down an abandoned chicken coop and an abandoned barn, not just because they were eyesores and hazards to public health, but because they were command bunkers for the Japanese General Staff. The barn burning was carried out with impeccable technique. We made maps of the area showing all relevant topographical features, we figured out where sentries should be posted, we estimated how long it would take to carry a can of gasoline from point A to point B and back. Before applying the match we sent patrols into the surrounding fields, we staged dress rehearsals, and for a solid weekend we crouched in a nearby woods with our eyes pressed to binoculars.

The fire was spectacular, to say the least, and it took every fireman in the county to keep it from spreading and to cope with blazes started blocks away by airborne sparks. All of us except Porky were shaken by how it almost got out of control and a couple of the guys went so far as to drop out of the gang, even though that put them in the "chicken" camp. Porky said that we couldn't stop now, that there were several more command posts that had to be taken care of. He pointed out that the skills we were learning would be of great value to our country later when we were in the branch of service of our choice. I was uneasy about the deep water we were getting into, but I didn't see how I could do anything about it. Besides, my brother was wounded now and needed my help. Our armed forces were making ever greater efforts, sensing final victory. Could Porky Schornhorst's Raiders do less?

2

One danger I had been faced with had, for the time being, receded—that of losing my soul by engaging in sexual perversions with Wanda Farney. She didn't go out with me until after the graduation dance, and my date with her didn't turn out as I had planned. Willie Richards hadn't broken up with her right away as he promised— apparently what he was doing with her was a habit hard to break. I took Ellen to the dance and tried to pretend she was Wanda, which didn't stop me from having a pretty good time. Ellen was very interesting to talk to and had lips that looked like they would be fun to kiss. She had a good time, too, and when we said goodnight she let me kiss her jaw. I was aiming for her lips but she turned her head at the last minute.

With Wanda things would be different, I was sure. A week or so after Willie had dropped her in favor of a cheerleader of his own faith, I found myself in a position I had imagined a thousand times in my dreams: on the front porch with Wanda, about to start the sequence of maneuvers destined to bring me a new understanding of the female body. She stood with her back to her front door looking at me, just as Willie said she would. I crossed my arms and looked casually at the ceiling as a first step toward putting my hands on her shoulders, after which I would express an interest in smelling the perfume in her hair, followed by a light kiss on the forehead, a heavier one on the cheek, and a really serious one on the mouth. But before I could make a move the porch light went on, the door opened, and there was the bald head of her father.

"Oh, it's you," he said.

Well, who the hell did you think it was?

"It's about time you were getting home, isn't it?" he said. "Did you have a nice time?"

"Yes," we both said.

"Do you two want to come in and listen to the radio with mother and me? H. V. Kaltenborn is on."

"No thanks," we said.

"All right, but I don't want you standing out there all night. Wanda, I want you inside in five minutes." To me he said, "Say hello to your folks for me, will you, Tommy?"

"I'll sure do that, Mr. Farney."

"Good. Five minutes, Wanda." He shut the door.

The evening was ruined now as far as I was concerned, and not just because Mr. Farney left the porch light on. The problem was that I couldn't see how I could put my hand between a girl's legs just after talking to her father. Wanda must have had the same feeling, because after watching me stare at the floor for a while she shrugged, said goodnight, and went inside.

On the way home I wondered if it was possible to do anything dirty to a girl if you so much as *knew* her father. Or her mother. Even if you married her, how could you do anything on your wedding night if you knew her mother and father? And if you didn't know them, you would know that she *had* a mother and father, and you would know that they weren't going to like the idea of some guy trying to push his big organ into their daughter's little place.

Maybe I would have to marry an orphan.

3

A few days after we got the letter from Paul I began working for the Milwaukee Railroad as a section hand, a job I thought would last all summer and for which I was magnificently ill-equipped. That I should have been hired at all is one of the little-known nightmares of World War II and illustrates the hardships and dislocations suffered by the civilian population during those dark years. The armed forces had vacuumed up almost every able-bodied adult male, leaving a severe labor shortage on the home front. By 1944 the railroads were reduced to forming section gangs out of kids fourteen to seventeen years old.

A job on the section was much sought after, even though all of the work was hot, heavy, and dirty, because it was considered manly and added greatly to your prestige as a tough guy and a lover. Before the war, summer jobs on the section were given only to those teen-agers who were football players at Crown of Thorns College or the University of Dubuque. My father always had a few athletes on his construction crews in the summer—husky kids who wanted the toughest pick and shovel jobs he had to offer.

I reported for work on a Monday morning, and it is convenient to trace the decline of American railroads from that moment. At fourteen I wasn't a physical specimen that would make a labor foreman rub his hands in anticipation; I was so skinny I could inflict puncture wounds with my elbows. But there I was, proudly standing with the big guys in my brand new steel-toed shoes and work gloves, ready to do my bit for the war effort and earn ninety-five cents an hour as well.

Our crew was an insult to the dignity of the labor movement. It took about forty of us all day to do what four experienced adults could have finished in an hour. We drove our old-time boss wild. When he looked the other way we would freeze in position and not move a muscle until he looked around again. We weren't as bad, though, as the teen-age gang working for the Illinois Central, which also had a generous sprinkling of stalwarts from St. Procopius. The boss left them one day to check the track around a bend and when he got back ten minutes later his entire work force was splashing in Catfish Creek, clothes strung out along the right-of-way. They got laid off for a week for that.

My first day on the job wasn't bad. I think the boss, a crusty old man with grey stubble named Charley Jack, didn't know what to make me do, as there wasn't anything on the site light enough for me to pick up. I walked around watching other people work, using a studious expression to imply that I was making a necessary preliminary survey of the various tasks and the best methods of doing them. For quite a while I watched a kid from the non-Catholic high school try to drive a spike into a creosoted wooden tie with a narrow-nosed sledge hammer. He swung amiably, raining blows on the rail, tie, and ballast near the spike. Every now and then he hit the spike a solid blow right on the head, which was a great satisfaction to both of us, but even on those happy occasions the spike didn't penetrate any discernible distance. He caught the hang of it after a time, and got so that he hit the spike at least a glancing blow oftener than he missed it—and even when he missed he came awfully close.

My survey of railroad-work techniques came to a sudden end on the third day. A group of us who hadn't been assigned anything were horsing around at the end of a bridge, dropping flat rocks into the water edgewise in an effort to decapitate a turtle, when Charley Jack's gravelly voice burst in our midst.

"Okay, you kids," he rasped. "I've got a job for you." He handed each of us a square-mouthed shovel and marched us off down the track like some far-fetched and hastily recruited platoon of rejects, which in fact we were. We looked at each other apprehensively when we arrived at Rafferty's Slough, a stagnant backwater of the Mississippi at the south end of town, where six empty cattle cars stood on a siding. We didn't know it then, but by the end of the day the nine of us, our shovels over our shoulders like toy muskets, would be known as the SS Squad, the SS standing for Shit Shovelers.

"The previous passengers on these Pullmans,"

Charley said with a jab of his thumb, "weren't too neat. In fact, they shit all over the floor. Now, we can't invite no new cows in there with the place looking like a pig sty, can we? No. So you fellas are going to clean them out. Climb right in and start shoveling. You should have these six done by tonight. Then I got six more for ya. Go on, move!"

We straggled toward the cars, our minds recoiling at what we had been told to do. We climbed slowly into them, our faces twisted in disbelief and revulsion.

"Don't act like a bunch of babies," Charley shouted. "These cars have got to be cleaned out, so get in there and clean them out. It's not so bad—you'll get used to it in no time. There's a war on, remember? We all gotta do stuff we don't like. Be thankful nobody's shooting at ya."

"You . . . you mean we're supposed to shovel it right into the water?" somebody asked.

Charley looked at the water, the green scum, the stumps, the half-submerged tires. "Yeah, that's right," he said. "Right in the water." He smiled a yellow, stumpy smile. "Don't worry, I won't make you drink any of it. Okay, now get busy." He turned and walked away, pausing for one final shot: "Anybody who don't like it can pick up his check at the office."

We watched his retreating figure for several minutes, accepting at last the fact that there was no joke involved, that we really were going to have to spend the day shoveling cowshit. We began to examine our new environment. Despite the open slat walls of the cattle cars, through which some light and air could enter, it was dark, dusty, and at least ten degrees hotter than outside. Thin sheets of sunlight sliced through the gloom at a steep angle, making us feel as though we were in a long, narrow cell with horizontal bars, a cell fit for a madman's dungeon.

4

The manure, we discovered with indescribable relief, was mostly dry, though there were lubricated spots here and there. It was in a fairly even layer four to six inches deep over the entire floor—apparently the constant vibration of the cars caused it to settle and pack solidly. We tested it tentatively and found that our shovels sank in easily. It actually was a good material to work with when you ruled out subjective and emotional factors. But they were not ruled out, and all of us were on the verge of throwing up for hours, even though we breathed through our mouths and carried our loads to the door with our faces turned toward the roof.

By the middle of the afternoon we had gotten more or less used to it. We were breathing normally, we were facing our work in order to waste no motion, and we were beginning to make a few jokes about our predicament. By quitting time we were even indulging in simple games, like throwing our shovelfuls in high trajectories so that they would plop into the green scum like depth charges.

On the opposite shore I saw a group of old men sitting on a log fishing for carp. At the far end of the slough, about a hundred yards away, some small children in swimming trunks were playing in the water. I paused for a moment, because it was a scene that made me realize how diversified and indomitable was the human spirit.

The day done, we marched up the line with a verve I never would have thought possible. Although our odor was enough to make your eyes water, there was a feeling of gaiety as we checked in our shovels at the tool shed and signed out with the timekeeper. The rest of the guys razzed us, of course, but we dished out as much as we took. We knew that we had survived one of the most horrible ordeals human beings had ever been subjected to, and that we were tougher and finer for it. So we were the SS Squad, were we? Okay. We would be the roughest, filthiest, meanest SS Squad in the whole goddam country.

The next day was great. We had completely lost our feelings of revulsion and fell to our work like so many hard-boiled soldiers of fortune who had seen and heard it all. The great part was that two of the cars had already been cleaned—by our counterparts in Davenport or Maquoketa—something Charley Jack hadn't noticed when he had them switched to the siding. This meant that we were able to spend a couple of hours sitting around on our asses doing nothing but smoking and cursing.

The following day was different. After checking in and getting our shovels, we trooped off to the slough in high spirits, spitting and exchanging the vulgarisms and rude gestures that had become our style. But as we neared the six cars that were waiting for us, our mood changed to uneasiness. Something was wrong. For one thing the smell was far, far worse. For another, these cars were double-deckers, which meant that they were used for pigs and sheep rather than cattle. Climbing aboard with growing dread, we found that we couldn't stand up straight on either level. We had to work stooped over and carry our loaded shovels to the door with a kind of duck walk. There were bolts sticking through the ceilings every few feet which gouged our backs the moment we forgot about them.

Worst of all was the condition of the manure itself. It hadn't been given a couple of days to dry out and lose its power. That stuff was *fresh!* It clung to our shovels and sucked at our shoes. The stink was so intense it drove the oxygen out of the air and penetrated directly into our minds and hearts. The subjective and emotional factors we thought we had ruled out came back with a rush. Our verve and our thick skins melted away as if they had never existed.

I was the first to break. I staggered to the door gasping for breath, fighting my stomach, and half climbed, half fell to the ground. I clung to the side of the car until an impulse to faint had passed, then I reeled away looking for Charley, my eyes full of tears and my legs like rubber.

After I had gone about a hundred yards into the fresh air my condition improved markedly. My head began to clear and my legs got stronger. Even my stomach calmed down. I hadn't thrown up; my nausea had been too profound for that.

5

By the time I found Charley I had made an almost complete recovery. He was supervising a long line of kids who were shoveling clean, dry, odorless gravel between the ties of a newly laid track.

"What the hell are you doing here?" he said when he saw me.

"I got sick," I said weakly. "I couldn't help it."

"Too fuckin' bad. Go get your check." He turned his back.

"Aw, gee, Mr. Jack," I said, "do you have to fire me? Isn't there something else I can do? I can work hard. Try me—you'll see how hard I can work." How would I be able to explain to my brother that I had been canned?

He turned around. "I can't to that," he said. "If I give you another job all those little bastards will be up here wanting something easier."

"Well, gee, I shoveled shit for two days . . . that's more than all these guys here. It's not fair. I'm willing to work."

He seemed to soften a little. He looked at me thoughtfully, like a dirty Lionel Barrymore. I think he understood my position and what I had been through. He must have shoveled shit himself when he was a boy. Finally he said: "What's your name?"

"Shannon."

"Gannon?"

"No, Shannon." I spelled it.

"Shannon?"

"Yes, sir."

"Your old man the one who put in the culvert out by the monastery?"

"Yes, sir."

"Well, I'll tell you what. I'll give you another chance. Been so many trains lately that Cinder Pit John is drowning in ashes. Maybe you could give him some help." He went into the tool shed and came out with a shovel for me that was hardly bigger than the kind that come with fireplaces. "See that coal car on the siding at the far end of the yard? That's where he works. Take this shovel and go over there and help him any way you can."

I thanked him profusely for the favor I thought he was doing me. I didn't dream that three days later, half dead from exhaustion and despair, I would be off the payroll and at home helping my mother fold the ironing.

Brilliant as my Uncle Ed was with a shovel, he was no match for Cinder Pit John when it came to sheer output. John worked in a long, narrow crypt under the tracks where the locomotives emptied their fireboxes. His job was to shovel the ashes into the coal car standing on the next track, which meant throwing them at least fifteen feet.

From the edge of the railroad yard you could see round piles of ashes popping out of the ground and sailing into the car as if they were clay pigeons pitched by a mechanical sling. If you listened intently you could hear the scrape of his big scoop on the concrete floor between each toss. The tempo of his movements never varied, hour after hour, week after week, year after year. Few people knew he existed; fewer had ever seen him in action.

When I first saw him I could hardly believe my eyes. I stood alongside the track and stared down at him, watching him work for several long minutes. He was like some kind of fantastic trained animal. Good God, I thought, the things people had to do to make a living!

Cinder Pit John was a short, burly man with powerful arms and shoulders. He had a broad face, with bushy eyebrows and a wide, thin mouth. His skin was dark, but it was impossible to tell how much of his color was due to the dust and soot that covered him. I couldn't even tell if he was Asian or European.

He didn't acknowledge my presence in any way, even though he must have seen me standing there. I lowered myself into the pit, throwing my shovel down first and hanging by my fingers from the rough edge of the concrete wall before dropping to the bottom.

6

The chamber was about ten feet wide and fifty feet long. A locomotive could thunder to a stop directly overhead and dump its ashes—half of them smoking and glowing red—at one end while John went on shoveling at the other. There was always the possibility that the ashes would be unloaded right on top of him, burying him like a potato in a campfire, but the engineers were careful not to do that; they knew there wasn't another shoveling machine like him anywhere in the world.

I walked toward him and stopped about six feet away. He went right on working as if I weren't there, although he glanced at me once with what could have been an expression of discomfort. I think he thought I was some sort of absurd apparition that would fade out sooner or later . . . who knows what images rose before him while laboring in that eerie and unknown hell?

I didn't know whether to introduce myself to him or not. It seemed wrong and maybe even dangerous to interrupt his rhythm, but it wasn't clear what I was supposed to do to help him. I was sure I couldn't throw any ashes into the car on the next track, the top of which towered impossibly high above me. Watching John do it with his giant scoop was awe-inspiring. He drove his shovel across the concrete floor into the bottom of the pile, lifted a heaping load, took two backward steps to get out from under the tracks, then in one movement turned to his left on the ball of his right foot, brought his arms to the right in a backswing and, with a large step, swung the shovel upward in a sudden arc. The ashes sailed with precision over the top edge of the car. Watching him do it from his own level was even more impressive than from above.

There was nothing for me to do but try it myself. I got a modest load in my shovel, swung my arms back, and threw it as high as I could. It was a serious mistake. The shovel flew out of my hands and only by making a desperate lunge did I deflect it from John as it came down. There was nothing I could do about the ashes—they landed on both of us like a cloudburst.

For the first time in history, Cinder Pit John stopped. He turned slowly and looked at me, his normally impassive mask betraying anger. I was real. I had to be dealt with.

"Go away," he said in a heavy accent.

"I'm supposed to help you," I told him. "Mr. Jack sent me down here to work. I guess I'm supposed to be sort of your assistant." I smiled as engagingly as I could.

He took several deep breaths and shook his head. Then he began to nod. Apparently he finally accepted me as one of those sudden reversals of fortune that sometimes come along in wartime.

"Okay," he said.

He showed me how to hold the shovel. He showed me where to stand for the best throwing angle and how to change my grip to maximize the leverage and control the aim. He made me practice the movements several times with an empty shovel. He used very few words, and those he did use I didn't understand. I decided from his accent that he was definitely some kind of European.

Eventually I built up enough confidence to try again. I managed to throw some ashes high enough so that they hit the side of the car about half way up . . . they ricocheted off and fell to the ground alongside the track. At least I got them out of the pit. My next try hit near the top, and my third was a complete success. "Oh, boy, did you see that one?" I said to John, who merely grunted and went back to his own work.

His indifference didn't make me any less pleased with myself. I spit on my gloves and attacked the ashes with vigor, determined to win his grudging approval and respect. But no matter how hard I tried, at least half my throws hit the side of the car. Every hour or so I climbed out and cleaned up the mess I had made.

The work was so bone-tiring I couldn't keep it up for long. To give my crying muscles some rest I tried to make John's work easier for him by cleaning the floor of debris near him, by loosening up the ashes in the pile he was working on, and by getting rid of any hot coals that might bother him. He took no notice of these attentions except to wave a hand at me when I got too close. I felt sure, though, that he was grateful for the help I was trying to give him.

During the second day, my strength and will

ebbing from me, I wondered if we would ever get to know each other. Perhaps if I kept on working hard he would eventually give me a look or a word of encouragement. Then someday, after our friendship had grown, he would invite me to come with him after work to a little room some-place where he lived, a room papered with pin-up girls and yellowed obituaries.

In what must have been the beginnings of de-lirium I imagined him making us some strong coffee and inviting me to sit down on one of the orange crates he used as chairs. As he gazed dis-tantly into the fumes rising from his cup, he would tell me vivid, poignant stories in broken English of his childhood in Croatia. . . .

But nothing like that ever happened. He didn't say hello when I came in the morning. He ate lunch alone. He didn't say goodbye when we parted at night. In the middle of the third day, when my body said the hell with it and refused to obey me anymore, and I climbed out of the pit for the last time, he didn't even look up. I said goodbye, but perhaps it was too feeble for him to hear. I dragged myself slowly toward Rhomberg Avenue, where I could catch a bus for home, dropping my shovel somewhere along the way.

We never saw each other again.

CHAPTER TWELVE

1

My mother noticed it first and fainted into my father's arms. Paul came toward us along the station platform on his crutches, thinner and straighter than I remembered him, a broad grin on his face, one leg bent slightly backward as if he were trying to avoid putting weight on a sprained ankle. He had so many ribbons on his chest it looked like the Flags of all Nations in the school encyclopedia. We waved and shouted when we saw him, and I ran for him as fast as I could, leaping over a pile of suitcases and dodging between the few other people who had gotten off the train. I almost jumped into his arms and let him swing me around the way he did before he went away, but I knew he was hurt and I managed to limit myself to a bear hug. He lifted me off the ground anyway, despite his crutches. We were both laughing and shouting.

"Holy Mackerel, Tommy," he said, "you've grown a foot since I've seen you . . . hey, what's the matter with mom?"

I looked back and saw dad holding mom up, shaking her lightly to bring her back to life. When she came to and saw Paul again she burst into tears and ran to him with her arms outstretched. Then we were all together, hugging each other, and asking Paul so many questions he didn't know which one to answer first. Dad rarely hugged anybody—just mom once a year on her birthday—but he hugged Paul that day. I think he kissed him, too, on the side of the head, but I couldn't tell for sure because mom was blocking my view. I don't think I had ever been so happy. I still hadn't noticed what made mom faint.

At the car dad insisted that mom and I sit in the back with Paul so we could both be next to him, that he didn't mind being in the front seat alone. We couldn't get in right away because there was a sack of cement and a bucket of nails in the back seat that had to be put in the trunk with the luggage. That was like old times and gave Paul a good laugh.

"Now I really know I'm home," he said. "There were a lot of times I wondered if I'd ever make it. Boy, the old town sure looks good."

"How long you going to be home for?" dad asked, applying a whisk broom to the back seat before we got in. "Just a few weeks, or what?"

"No, dad, I'm afraid you're stuck with me for longer than that. Medical discharge. The army doesn't have too much use for a guy with only one foot."

Till that moment I had hardly been able to take my eyes off Paul's face, but I looked down then and saw it . . . or rather, didn't see it. At the end of the left leg of his neatly pressed trousers there was no foot . . . there was nothing there, just a round, black hole. My brother had lost his foot.

It was my turn to cry. As we drove up Dodge Street I turned my face into the ribbons on his chest and covered them with tears, while he held me tightly with an arm around my shoulders. My crying somehow enabled my mother to recover her strength. Holding his free hand in both of hers, she looked at him with a happy-sad face while he told us how it happened.

"You're going to come out of this," my father said several times while Paul talked. "You're going to be all right."

"I was riding in a jeep with five other guys," Paul said, "and we hit a mine. Two of the guys got killed. I got it in the foot, but it didn't seem too bad. They shipped me back to Sicily. It kept getting worse . . . infection. About a month ago they had to take it off. I couldn't tell you— you know that, mom—you would have worried yourself to death. I told you about the crutches so you would at least be prepared for something. Now let's not talk about it any more, okay? It doesn't hurt and the artificial foot they are fixing for me is so good that nobody will be able to tell anything, once I get used to it. Now, how about answering a few of *my* questions. . . ."

All the praying my mother had done to keep my brother safe! What good had it done? If God didn't answer my mother's prayers, did He answer anybody's? All of the feats I had performed at night, all my daydreams, all of the trouble I had gone to and the risks I had taken . . . all wasted, all for nothing. My brother had lost his foot. Nothing we had done for the last two years had helped at all.

2

It was amazing how well people treated my brother, even people who had never seen him before. All servicemen were treated well, but a heavily decorated soldier on crutches with only one foot? He could have run for mayor and won in a landslide. He found it impossible to pay for a bottle of pop or a glass of beer. He couldn't walk more than thirty feet down the street without having someone offer him a ride. Some of the best-looking girls in town, including one who had a convertible, came to our house in their cars to take him to movies and parties. When he visited St. Procopius one afternoon the nuns and priests fell all over him, apparently forgetting that he had been far from a model student and in fact had almost been kicked out of school once for taking a bottle of whiskey on a basketball trip.

The guys in my gang made a fuss over him, too. They pressed around him, asked him to explain every ribbon and medal he had, and begged him to tell them about his heroic exploits, practically inviting him to make up some tall tales, which they promised by their faces to believe. But for a couple of weeks he wouldn't tell us anything important. He told some funny stories about barracks life, the food he had to eat, and the characters in his outfit, but nothing about action. We were patient, having discovered already that soldiers back from the war had to be given a little time to settle down before they would talk about any of the juicy stuff.

Paul finally told us a story, and when he had finished we wished we hadn't coaxed him. Porky was there, and so were most of the other guys in the gang, standing around in front of Corrigan's Drug Store waiting for the sky to get dark. When Paul came out of the store, where he had spent an hour talking with Mr. and Mrs. Corrigan, we all greeted him. Somebody asked him what invading Italy was like.

"It wasn't very much like you think it was," he said after a pause. That's when he told us a story that left us all white as sheets. He had been caught in sniper fire, he said, and he and another guy had to dive into a ditch. There was a dead German soldier lying in the water at the bottom and the smell was sickening. They had to stay there for two days because whenever they raised their heads they drew rifle shots. They couldn't even crawl out to go to the toilet. The other guy finally went crazy, and blew himself up with a grenade, covering my brother with gore. Paul jumped out of the trench then and stumbled across the countryside all night before finding the American lines.

My brother took no pleasure in telling us this.

He was very grim, and had a hard time finishing. He spoke slowly, pausing between every sentence as if trying to teach us something. What the hell it was he was trying to teach us I don't know, but if he was trying to turn our stomachs he succeeded. When he swung around on his crutches and went slowly down the sidewalk, everybody stared after him with sick expressions and open mouths. Mule Kahlbach put his hands on the radiator of his car and threw up all over it.

I went home early and didn't sleep all night.

3

A few days later I got another shock. I overheard my brother and my mother talking about me. It was strictly an accident, even though I often eavesdropped on purpose.

I had left the house after supper to join the gang. Porky had an ambitious plan to block the highway, and this was the night we were supposed to do it. We had discussed it, mapped it, and practiced it so often that everybody knew his assignment by heart. It involved chopping down a telephone pole ("an enemy observation tower," Porky called it) so it would fall across the road. Special suicide squads were then supposed to let the air out of the tires of the squad cars that came to the rescue. That was the plan, but I didn't show up to play my part.

About a block from my house I became aware of not wanting to go through with it. It wasn't that I was afraid, it was just that there seemed to be no point in it. Blocking traffic—what the hell good would that do anybody? The whole idea of Porky Schornhorst's Raiders began to strike me as foolish. All of the things the gang had done, had they protected my brother? No. I found myself not walking; I was simply standing on the sidewalk staring into space. The spirit seemed to have drained out of me. I don't know why I suddenly felt so useless and defeated, but I suppose it had something to do with the thoughts that were turning over endlessly in my mind: the story Paul had told us, the missing foot at the end of his leg, the hundreds of rosaries my mother had said that God had chosen to ignore. Whatever the reasons were, I couldn't develop any interest in letting air out of tires. I couldn't turn my mind to it all. Maybe some other night.

Hands in my pockets and shoulders drooping, I walked aimlessly back toward the house. Maybe my brother and mother and I could listen to the radio, or make fudge, or work on a jigsaw puzzle. Dad was at the Legion, so we couldn't play euchre.

As I came up the front yard I heard my brother's voice floating out of the open dining room window. I stopped and listened.

". . . what he's doing tonight? Do you have any idea?"

He was talking about me and his voice was angry. I didn't hear my mother's reply.

"That's just the trouble," Paul said. "You don't know. He could be anywhere. He could be doing anything. Have you met those numskulls he hangs around with? Almost every one of them is older than he is. . . ."

"They're all from St. Procopius, aren't they?" I heard my mother say in a defensive voice. "They couldn't be *too* bad. . . ."

"Like hell they couldn't." I had never heard Paul say "hell" to my mother, but he seemed very upset, and the worst was yet to come. "Have you met the Callahan kid? With the big ears? He spends most of his time seeing how much noise he can make passing wind. And Porky Schornhorst? Have you had the pleasure of meeting General Porky Schornhorst, world's greatest military authority and juvenile delinquent? That kid is headed for jail or I miss my guess. That's where Tommy is going to end up, too, if he doesn't watch out, or if he doesn't get some new friends. I'm telling you, ma, that gang of his is a bigger threat to public safety around here than Bullets Ghilloti ever was. You and dad have got to step in and do something. If you don't I will." Paul had been pretty quiet since he'd been home, but he sure wasn't being quiet now. I stood under the window with my ears wide open.

"Well I had no idea," my mother said. "I guess Leonard and I will have to have a talk with him."

"Talking isn't enough, ma! Something has got to be done! I saw the nuns and they told me he's been in trouble they haven't told you about. Haven't you noticed his grades? Nothing but C's all year. He's smarter than that."

"What should we do?" said my mother, beginning to sob a little. "It's been hard here with you away and Leonard at that rotten Legion almost every night. . . ."

"Don't start crying, for chrissakes! That's not going to solve anything. I'll tell you what has to be done. Get Tommy out of St. Procopius. That place is hopeless. The nuns have most of those kids so screwed up it's a crime. You know who Tommy had for a teacher all last year? Sister Raphael. I had her when I was in eighth grade and I'll bet she's worse now than she was then. She thinks it's a sin to say hocus-pocus. Honest to God! She thinks that if you get caught in a blizzard all you have to do is say a rosary. I tell you, ma, it takes more than a rosary to get along in this world . . . I've been out there . . . I've seen it. If all I had was a rosary in Italy, I'd be a dead duck now, I'll tell you that."

"Take Tommy out of St. Procopius? Where would we send him?"

"Dubuque Central. They have teachers there who have been to college. I know, I know, it's not a Catholic school, but don't look at me as if I said he should give up his religion. He can always go to Crown of Thorns or Notre Dame later. But he's got to go to a high school now where he will learn something. Get him out of St. Procopius before he's ruined completely. That place is no good. It's like a nuthouse."

"Oh, Paul, how can you say that? Your own school? We can't send Tommy to Central . . . Father Grundy would never. . . ."

"Fuck Father Grundy! Aw, gee, ma, I'm sorry . . . I didn't mean to say that. I've been with some awful rough guys the last couple of years and it's hard to clean up my language all of a sudden. Forget what I just said. It's just that we have to put Tommy ahead of Father Grundy. All Father Grundy cares about is the building fund. This thing with Tommy is serious. We'll talk about it tomorrow with dad—he should take more of an interest in this. I think I can convince him that a change has got to be made before Tommy gets into some real big trouble. Come on, mom, cheer up. Let's turn on the radio. It's about time for Gabriel Heatter."

4

"Tommy, is that you?"

"Yes, mom." I had been walking the streets for almost three hours and it was past midnight. The house was dark and I had tiptoed in as quietly as I could, but there was no way of getting into my room without my mother knowing it.

"Where have you been? It's awfully late."

"Sorry, mom. I met some guys and we got to talking and I lost track of the time. Paul asleep?"

"No, Carl Breitbach came by and they went out. I suppose they're over in East Dubuque somewhere." She was standing in the doorway of my room, her hair in curlers and her face covered with cold cream. "I wish you would stay home more," she said. "I get worried, not knowing where you are or what you are doing, and your father down at that dirty, rotten, stinking Legion

208

night after night. What if you got hit by a car or fell off a cliff? Then what would I do? I don't think I could take it. . . ."

"Nothing is going to happen to me," I said, sitting on the edge of the bed taking off my shoes. "Everything is fine. Dad will be home soon. You go to bed. There's nothing to worry about."

She sighed. "Nothing to worry about . . . it's been a long time since I could say that. It's easy for you, at your age. Life is so simple for you. Wait till you're as old as I am—then you'll know what worry is. I just hope that your kids are as good as you are and stay out of trouble."

"Yeah. Well, good night, mom. Have a good night's sleep."

She was looking at me wistfully as I put on my pajamas and I was afraid she was going to come over and hug me and kiss me. She was a swell mother, but I hated it when she did that. It wasn't too bad when we were alone, but sometimes she forgot herself and did it when my friends were around.

"Should I tuck you in?"

"No thanks. I'm fourteen. Good night."

"Good night, Tommy." She turned out the light and softly closed the door.

I was tired and as my head sunk into my pillow I wanted very much to go to sleep and forget about my problems, but my brain kept working, going over and over everything that had happened since Paul had come back. I had walked all the way to Eagle Point Park that night and had relived every hour, but still I couldn't figure anything out or decide what I should do. I kept thinking of what he had said about my going to Central. How could he want me to do that? I thought he hated Central as much as anybody at St. Procopius—I know he did when he was in school and the teams he played on were getting drubbed by them. I tried to imagine myself sitting in the Dubuque Central cheering section, but I couldn't. Still, it would be nice having players like Spider Oglethorpe on your team . . . and it would be nice getting away from some of those weird nuns. . . .

My prayers! Goddammit, I had forgotten to kneel down and say my prayers. I didn't have the energy to get up—I would have to say them lying down or not at all. Hail Mary, full of grace, the Lord is with thee, blessed art thou amongst women, and blessed is the fruit of thy womb, Jesus. . . . As I said the words in my mind, images began to swim before me like great, shadowy sea creatures, images of Bernice Vorwald. . . . Holy Mary, Mother of God, pray for us sinners, now and at the hour of our death, amen. Go away, Bernice. I don't want to think about you. Hail Mary, full of grace . . . if I think about anybody I want to think of Gretchen, who may be clinging to the drainpipe right now . . . or of Ellen and her clear eyes and her heart-shaped lips . . . or of Wanda Farney and what it would be like to slip my hand beneath the elastic on her panties. Blessed is the fruit of thy womb . . . Bernice, will you please get out of my room? I've got to say my prayers and do some serious think-

210

ing. I know you're only trying to help, poor, fat, faithful Bernice, but . . . oh, all right, one little kiss goodnight . . . why, Bernice! You don't have any clothes on! And who's that with you? Gretchen? Gretchen, you *did* come! And Wanda! Oh, God, not all of you at once . . . can't a couple of you come back another time? I'm so tired . . . you can't wait? Okay, climb in . . . throw your clothes anywhere, the room's a mess already. Snuggle up in my arms and make yourselves comfortable, but don't touch me Down There until I've said my prayers. Oh, that feels good! Everybody is so warm and soft . . . just lie quietly for a minute while I finish my prayers and then we'll see what happens. Hail Mary . . . Hail . . . hail . . .

> . . . the gang's all here;
> What the hell do we care,
> What the hell do we care;
> Hail, hail, the gang's all here,
> What the hell do we care now?

> "Jumpy, kinetic, and finally very powerful, a deeply felt piece of work by a very gifted young writer."
> —Joan Didion

LITHIUM FOR MEDEA

KATE BRAVERMAN

☐ 41-185-5 $2.75

Originally published in hardcover to nationwide critical acclaim, here is the poignant story of a volatile young woman who becomes entangled in a web of immobilizing unhappiness and desperate drug addiction when the pressure—and paranoia—of loved ones reaches unbearable dimensions.

> "Moving and absorbing."—*Publishers Weekly*
> "An intense, beautifully written novel."
> —*The Boston Globe*
> "A piece of writing that will shake you."
> —*Rolling Stone*
> "Difficult to put down."—*Los Angeles Herald-Examiner*

More Best-Selling Fiction from Pinnacle